Your*Shift*Matters

Compiled by Dana Zarcone

Resistance to RESILIENCE

For more information, visit:

Compiler / Publisher: www.danazarcone.com

Writing coach/Proofreading - Suzanne LaVoie: www.suzannelavoiewrites.com

Cover design - Amanda: www.letsgetbooked.com

Editing - Amanda: www.letsgetbooked.com

Formatting - Bojan Kratofil: www.expertformatting.com

ISBN: 978-1-5136-4133-1

Gratitude

First and foremost, I'd like to take this opportunity to thank the amazing authors of this book! I have been in awe of the passion, grace and courage all of you have shown. I couldn't be more blessed or grateful to have been on this journey with you. You've put your heart into the pages of this book in the spirit of inspiring others through your story. I've read each and every page, and I know that you will touch the hearts of so many readers around the world. I am so very proud of you.

Frankly, I found it so mind blowing that so many of you knew each other before hopping on board, yet you didn't know you'd be co-authors at the time. To me, this was evidence that the Universe works in mysterious ways, and that we were all meant to be together on this journey.

The energy you've put into this book, and the passion you put into this project, has made this book one of my favorites. During the project, I've had some personal challenges with two deaths in my immediate family, both of which came about unexpectedly. I'll be forever grateful for the outpouring of love and support that you gave to me during this very challenging time. Your open hearts and loving energy were greatly appreciated.

I also want to express my gratitude to my production team. Your strong conviction and willingness to pick up the slack while I spent time with my family was priceless. As you know, it's important to keep these projects moving along. It would've come to a grinding halt without you. Thank you very much. I am so grateful to each and every one of you. We've become a 'well-oiled machine', and it is shows in the quality of the finished product. I can't wait to deliver this book to the world. The graphics rock, the stories are amazing, and the impact will be felt far and wide!

Finally, I want to thank my father for his unwavering faith in me as a daughter, mother, coach, author, and publisher. When I was younger, my parents used to warn me about burning the candle at both ends. They said I would burn out if I kept taking too much on at one time. Fortunately, that's still how I roll, and I wouldn't have it any other way! Thanks, Dad, for always having my back. For loving me, guiding me and, well, grounding me when I needed it most.

My genuine love to each and every one of you. I look forward to the many adventures we are sure to have in the future.

Table of Contents

Introduction

Welcome to the Your Shift Matters book series! A series that was born to inspire, motivate and move you in ways you've never felt before. This compilation brings authors together from all walks of life, and all over the world, who share raw and real stories of overcoming unimaginable challenges, rising strong, and learning many lessons along the way. Their stories are sure to challenge your mind, touch your heart, and ignite your spirit.

When I started my Your Shift Matters podcast, I never thought in a million years that it would lead me down this powerful path of publishing. The overarching message of my brand is that you have to deal with your shit in order to make a shift! I'm passionate about this because so many people suffer, stay stuck, and live unhappy lives for no other reason than they refuse to deal with their shit! Are you one of them? If so, you're living in resistance.

I was guilty of this for a very long time. I'm sure my authors have been guilty of this as well. Instead of dealing with the issue—or perhaps more importantly—the pain associated with the issue, we resist it. As a result, everything is swept under the rug or pushed aside in hopes it will all go away; it won't.

I've seen and experienced a lot of suffering, as have the authors of this book. I'm certain you've experienced your fair share of suffering as well. This breaks my heart because it doesn't have to be this way! We aren't meant to suffer. We're supposed to feel vibrantly alive; resonating with love, joy, and compassion. We're meant to live a fulfilling, meaningful life. Yet, the majority of us don't live this way.

In this book, the authors will unveil their suffering to you. They have shared their stories of adversity, facing tough challenges, overcoming resistance and becoming resilient. They will bring you along on their journey and share with you the pain, heartbreak, grief, sorrow, and suffering they've endured.

Why on earth would people put their pain and suffering in a book for all the world to see!? Because they want you to understand that you're not alone. That we all experience tough times in our lives, and that it's not the tough times that matter as much as how you handle them.

Their stories will inspire you and give you hope. They will give you a sense of knowingness that if they can overcome the pain they've had to endure, and let go of resistance, so can you!

I invite you to read each story without judgment; with an open heart and genuine compassion. By approaching each chapter with an open mind, you'll find a little bit of yourself in each one. You'll realize that you can't fully embrace life when you're experiencing resistance. You'll learn that only by letting go of the resistance can you become resilient and embrace all that life has to offer!

Are you ready to make a change?

It's through my podcast, this book, and the amazing stories the authors share that you'll find the hope, inspiration, and the resilience to do what you need to do create your kick-ass, epic life!

Remember, at the end of the day, in order to live your life all-in and full-out, Your Shift Matters!

With lots of heartfelt love and gratitude,

Dana Zarcone, MSCC, NCC, CEP

Leadership & Success Coach | 4X #1 Bestselling Author & Publisher | Speaker | Podcast Host

www.danazarcone.com

Dana Zarcone

Dana is passionate about guiding her clients, so they can live all-in and full-out, step into their power, and enjoy epic success in life and business. She accomplishes this by helping her clients make significant shifts in their lives through coaching and making those shifts matter by publishing their stories so they can inspire others.

Following a successful twenty-four-year corporate career, Dana earned her Master's in Community Counseling. She's a national board-certified counselor, certified Core Energetics practitioner, and a certified energy healer and coach.

Dana integrates neuroscience, quantum physics, kinesiology, and psychology to show her clients what is truly possible. Through her broad range of education, research, and experience, Dana has developed a novel approach that has helped hundreds of clients make measurable, positive shifts in their lives.

Dana provides local and virtual services that include experiential workshops, training classes, and individual and group coaching. In addition, she's a highly sought-after motivational speaker, 4X international #1 bestselling author and publisher, and host of the *Your Shift Matters* podcast.

Find Dana online:

www.DanaZarcone.com
www.YourShiftMatters.com
www.Twitter.com/DanaZarcone

A Resilient Legacy

By Dana Zarcone

Becoming aware of our own mortality can be a liberating experience. However, studies have shown that when people contemplate their mortality, it generates feelings of fear and anxiety. However, when they come face to face with it, they become more grateful, realizing so much of their life has been taken for granted. I've had my own experiences that have made a huge impact on my life. After this year, in particular, I will forever be changed.

I took my daughters to go see my family in New Mexico for the Fourth of July this year. We don't get out there very often, so they were very excited to see my side of the family again. I was excited to see them as well, as I had really missed them. Especially my brother Mitch who, for some unknown reason, decided he didn't want to have contact with me. Up until about a year ago, we hadn't spoken for almost two years. This would be the first time in years I'd get to be with him. No white elephant in the room, no awkward tension. Just our normal selves again. I couldn't wait to see him!

The whole family gathered together several times during our visit. However, the most treasured experience was when I got together with just my siblings. My two older brothers, my sister-in-law and my younger sister. The time we all spent together that night will always be cherished. We reminisced, laughed, got serious, and then repeated the process. We'd never been together like that before…just the five of us.

At the time, we also wanted to get together to support my sister, whose health is failing. We wanted her to know she didn't have to be alone. That we're here for her. In her typical stubborn 'I can handle it' style, we didn't get very far. She's always been headstrong like that. I was happy we tried though because, on some level, I know she was able to feel our love and support.

After my sister and oldest brother left, I stayed for a while, talking with my brother, Mitch, and my sister-in-law, Dee Dee. The house had become quiet. There was a calm in the room that I was really enjoying. I had a great talk with them that I hadn't experienced in a very long time. When I left, I gave them a hug and said goodbye. What I didn't know when I left their house that night is that it would be the last conversation I would ever have with Mitch. When I flew back home, I was unaware that everything was about to change.

Just a week later, he was diagnosed with metastasized melanoma. When I was there, he wasn't feeling 100%, and they thought it was his gall bladder, which they were supposed to remove. They never removed it. They found that his melanoma had metastasized into his liver, spleen, and spine. Weeks went by, and the news continued to get worse. It eventually spread into his lungs, his bones, and who knows where else. Needless to say, this was aggressive, and it was spreading fast.

I hated being so far away. I felt helpless and desperate. I wanted nothing more than to be there to support him as he was going through one of the most challenging times of his life. I wanted to be there for him and the rest of my family. *What right do I have not to bear any of the burden that my family is going through!?* I felt horrible...helpless! *Will I ever see him again? Will he get better? Surely this is some tragic nightmare!*

Dee Dee had lost her brother two years ago, so she had a good idea what I was going through. She promised me that if it got really bad, she'd call me and tell me when it was time for me to come back home. Unfortunately, that call would come just six weeks later. I hopped on a plane and headed back to New Mexico.

When I saw him for the first time, it took all my energy to hold back the tears. My throat constricted, like I was being choked. I felt this heaviness in the pit of my stomach as if I was going to throw up. The weight in my chest was so overwhelming I could hardly breathe. *No, this can't really be happening! Please let me wake up and realize this is just a horrible dream!*

I stayed for an entire week, spending all my time with family...mostly Mitch. He was too weak to speak most of the time, much less carry on a conversation. Instead, he'd use hand gestures in response to what was being said. From time to time he'd open his eyes trying to be more present in the conversation. He was being fed through a nasogastric tube (NG tube). After each 'meal' he'd have to sit up for an hour. It was then that I'd steal one-on-one time with him.

The first night I was there, I sat with him, grabbed his hand and asked him how he was doing. His response broke my heart. "Why is this happening to me? I don't understand why this is happening to me!" It was at that moment I probably felt the most helpless.

Why? Because I didn't have an answer for him! I wish I did, but I didn't. Nobody did.

Just a few days later, he ended up back in the hospital. He was losing this battle, and he was suffering tremendously. I oscillated between the sadness I felt at the possibility of losing him forever and the deep pain I felt as I watched him lying there suffering. Nobody should ever experience the intense suffering he had to endure. Nobody.

On my last day there, I spent hours with him. As time ticked by, I got more and more tense. I knew that leaving him would be one of the most difficult things I've ever had to do. *Damn it! It was time! I have to go!* Once again, I choked back the tears trying not to break down in front of him. I reached over and gave him a kiss on the forehead, and I said, "I love you, Mitch." Miraculously he said, "I love you too." I walked out of that room overwhelmed with sadness and grief. I knew in my heart that would be the last time I'd see him. I cried the entire forty-minute ride home, struggling to see the road through the endless flow of salty tears.

Getting on that plane to go back home wasn't any easier. As we picked up speed and started to lift off the ground, I looked back at the horizon knowing my visits there would always be different now. Things would never be the same. Just a week later, my sister-in-law called me to tell me he had passed. It was the most gut-wrenching, heart-crushing, painful experience I've ever had to endure. I was devastated. I went into my back yard, walked deep into the woods and wailed out loud, "No! You can't leave me now! We just got back on track! Why the *fuck* did you just leave me? I need you, Mitch! *I need you!*" I was in a state of total panic, as I begged and pleaded with him to come back.

From diagnosis to death, it was less than eight weeks. Eight weeks of pure hell for him, for his wife and kids...for all of us. Things happened so fast, there was no time to process it, much less make any sense of it all. A beautiful soul gone way too soon, he was about to turn fifty-six.

His death, while tragic, had a huge impact on me. I observed a lot of resistance and resilience as the events unfolded. My brother was the poster child for resilience through all of this. While he questioned why this was happening to him, he never complained once. Sure, he got agitated from time to time, but he never complained. In fact, through this entire process, he was the *bravest* one of all of us.

He was a stellar example of making a shift from resistance to resilience. Initially, he had conviction, and there was no way he was going down without a fight. As time passed, and his level of suffering intensified, he consciously made the most difficult decision I think anyone could ever make. He said he wanted to leave the hospital and go home. He didn't want to be poked and prodded anymore. He didn't want to fight anymore. He wanted to leave this earth on his terms. He was questioned many times, and each time his answer was the same. "I'm not afraid to die. I understand the decision I'm making. I'm ready to go." A prime example of what it means to be resilient.

The thought of dying scares most of us. What comes afterward is the one thing that none of us really understands. The 'great unknown' is something we all fear on some level. In order to calm these fears, we create philosophical, spiritual or religious beliefs that we hold on to in order to find peace in the thought of our passing. But none of us *really know*.

The one thing I *do* know is that death is a wakeup call for those of us left behind on this earth. Those of us that take each breath for granted. Most of us aren't really living at all. We're pretending to live when, deep down, we feel empty, dissatisfied, and numb. We resist life. We're all lucky enough to be here, and we don't even appreciate it. We live our lives as if we have all the time in the world, but we don't.

I've had several of my own brushes with death. Not the kind where my heart stopped, the paddles were charged, and I was floating up by the ceiling looking down on myself. However, they were 'close calls' that scared the bejeezus out of me and caused me to grapple with my own mortality. Let's just say they were 'near death' enough!

When I was three, I was quarantined in an oxygen tent due to haemophilus influenza, a very invasive bacterial disease. My prognosis was bleak. They didn't think I would pull through. Seven years later, I was diagnosed with Reye's syndrome, which causes serious swelling in the liver and brain, and my parents were told I wouldn't make it. At the time, there were only thirteen cases in the US, and only two of us lived. Since then, I've been blasted out of an exploding speedboat, I've run out of air at 130 feet underwater, I've been stung by an extremely venomous scorpion, and hit by a car and airlifted to a head trauma center with a severe concussion. (Needless to say, I love playing 'two truths and a lie'!)

I'd be remiss not to mention something else. It wasn't a 'close call' like the others. This one crept up on me – bit by bit, day by day, and month by month. This was about six years ago when I ended up on the cold tile of a bathroom floor begging God to bring me home. I was done. I was in tremendous pain—physically, mentally, and emotionally. I couldn't take it anymore. I just wanted to go home. "Please, dear God, just bring me home!"

It was at that moment I hit my personal rock bottom…and I hit it hard!

Looking back, I suppose it's no surprise this happened. I was the poster child for someone living in resistance. Over the years, I ignored the warning signs and symptoms—the alarm bells that were going off that eventually got louder and louder until they could no longer be ignored, much less silenced.

When I collapsed on the bathroom floor that night, it wasn't due to a chemical imbalance in my brain. I didn't have a disease. The reality is that I was depressed because I was living in resistance. When you're living in resistance, the demons and dragons sit on the sidelines, watching and waiting for the perfect time to rear their ugly heads. As the saying goes, you can run, but you can't hide. Eventually, it catches up to you.

I felt ashamed that I got to that point. Since I had all of those 'close calls', I always felt that it was God's way of telling me that He had big plans for me. That I had a unique purpose in life that I needed to fulfill. I believed it with all my heart. However, over time, something was wrong. Something was really wrong. I didn't feel that I was on the right path at all.

Over time I zigged and I zagged, excelling at everything I set out to do. I was an over-achieving, ambitious perfectionist. While that can serve you well sometimes, most of the time it is a huge liability, and I was no exception to this. I followed the plan that was set in motion by my parents, and my intention was to exceed their expectations…which I did.

I got my college degree, landed an exceptional job and great salary with a Fortune 100 company, and climbed that proverbial corporate ladder. By most standards, I was really successful.

Successful or not, I wasn't truly happy. Why? Because I did it for all the wrong reasons. I did it so I would be loved and accepted. I did it so my parents wouldn't be disappointed in me. I did it so others would think highly of me. I was living my life according to what other's expected of me, never taking into account what *I* really wanted.

Honestly, collapsing on the bathroom floor was my turning point. It was my wakeup call that something was horribly wrong. I had no sense of self, and my personal power lay dormant. I couldn't be happy because I denied my heart and was overwhelmed with piles of unhealed emotions, limiting core beliefs, visceral fears, and a lot of resistance. Of course, I didn't know this at the time! I had to do some real soul searching and deep work to realize my modus operandi. Ultimately, what I figured out was that I was living my life based on 'resume virtues'.

My oldest brother did the eulogy at Mitch's service. He talked about this very concept. He spoke about living your life according to 'resume virtues' or 'eulogy virtues'. This is a concept introduced in *The Moral Bucket List* by David Brooks.

What this boils down to is how you live your life and how you want to be remembered after you're gone. Would you rather be remembered for the letters in front of your name, the figures on your paycheck, the size of your house or the type of car you drive? Or would you rather be remembered for the legacy you leave behind as a result of your compassion, kindness, humility, wisdom, courage, and integrity? Would you rather wear a mask, pretending to be someone you're not, solely focused on the superficial means with which to impress others? Or would you rather embrace all of who you are—no excuses, no apologies—knowing the world is a better place because you were once here?

As I sat and listened to the comparison, I realized that when we are living according to 'resume virtues' we are in resistance. It's a narcissistic approach to life where we are guarded, insecure and so afraid of getting hurt that we focus on the superficial things in life.

When you're living according to 'resume virtues' you withhold love, refuse to forgive, and blame, criticize and judge others. You are a victim. Your modus operandi is to impress people so you can feel accepted and loved, when deep down you feel the opposite. You really feel depressed, stressed, and overwhelmed. You're riddled with feelings of guilt, shame, fear, anger, and pride. You approach every day haphazardly and unintentionally. If you were to die today, you'd have a lot of regrets and unfinished business.

Conversely, when we are living according to 'eulogy virtues' we are exhibiting resilience. It's an empowered approach to life where we are confident and grounded in who we are. When you live according to 'eulogy virtues', you live your life unapologetically. You're kind, gentle and loving to yourself and others. You take full responsibility for the life that you live, knowing it's a culmination of what's within you. You aren't afraid to feel the pain. In fact, you welcome it and the lessons it brings. Your modus operandi is to be authentic and make everyone around you feel good about themselves. You resonate with feelings of love, compassion, courage, and acceptance. You approach every day intentionally, living your life on purpose. When your time comes, you have no regrets, no ill will, and no unfinished business because you lived each day as if it were your last. You can leave with a sense of peace knowing you fulfilled your purpose here on earth.

I know now that all of those 'close calls' were just other wake up calls in disguise. Ever since I collapsed on the bathroom floor that night, 'resume virtues' haven't mattered to me much. Instead, I've embraced 'eulogy virtues', and it has changed my life. Now I am confident and grounded in who I am. I no longer hold myself in contempt for my wrongdoings. I live my life unapologetically, with compassion for myself and others. I know in my heart those 'close calls' were messages from a higher power reminding me that I do have a purpose here on earth. I am a powerful, confident woman that is meant to be a catalyst for change. (Hence, the purpose of this book series.) I have gifts that I no longer suppress but, instead, I embrace. I choose to live my life intentionally, so I can fulfill my purpose. I choose to live by 'eulogy virtues'.

I can say unequivocally that my brother, Mitch, lived according to 'eulogy virtues' as well. He was a man of amazing integrity. With Mitch, you always knew where you stood. He was a no B.S., 'you get what you get' kind of guy. He was a great brother, amazing father, loving husband and a loyal friend. He touched thousands of lives during his twenty-one years as a teacher.

I'm so proud of him! He made the shift from resistance to resilience most eloquently. He was so brave to make the choice that he made. Because he lived his life the way he did, he was able to hear God's calling and leave this earth with a sense of peace. He left an amazing legacy that will impact many generations to come.

What about you? What kind of legacy will you leave? Will you be remembered for how impressive and important you are? Or will you be remembered for the lives you touched, the impact you had and the people you've inspired along the way? Will you live according to 'resume virtues' or 'eulogy virtues'?

When the alarm goes off tomorrow, will you get up begrudgingly—knowing you're about to face a daily grind that will suck the life out of you? Or will you get up with enthusiasm, curiosity, and excitement knowing that today's the day! The day you're going to make your mark on the world. The day you're going to live as if it were your last…because it just might be.

Jan Firstenberg

After a successful business career, Jan was inspired to earn multiple holistic certifications that resulted in her becoming an ordained interfaith minister and launching her private holistic energy practice in Manhattan in 2006.

Her main certifications include Eden Energy Medicine (by Donna Eden), Emotional Freedom Technique (EFT, by Gary Craig), Quantum Energy Transformation (QET by Joshua Bloom), and Therapeutic Energy Kinesiology (TEK, by Dr. Adrian Brito-Babapulle). Jan's extensive training in a broad base of energy protocols, along with her seminary training, has taught her the critical skills of active listening, being present, and trusting intuition.

In addition to her practice, Jan has taught classes, published articles, been a speaker for organizations, and is an emotional assistant for Dr. Dawson Church (head of EFT Universe), and a teaching assistant for Donna Eden.

Find Jan online:

https://www.janfirstenberg.com/
https://www.janfirstenberg.com/Healing-Modalities.html
https://www.facebook.com/jan.firstenberg

From Victim to Victorious

By Jan Firstenberg

Growing Up

Despite coming from a loving family, I was a lonely, fearful, extremely sensitive child. My parents, Sophie and Eddie, were kind and very outgoing, with lots of friends. My older brother, Barry was very popular in school, while my younger sister, Wendy, was the baby who screamed for, and received, everyone's attention. She, too, was popular.

I was the stereotypical neglected middle child. I was overweight, stuttered very badly, had a few facial tics, and was extremely shy. I knew I was loved by my family, but I was 'different' than the rest of them. When a sad movie came on, they all would gawk at me and say, "Look at Janis—she's crying."

My family was noisy, carrying on with lots of yelling and screaming (arguments about little things that everyone but me forgot about afterward). I always felt the need to make peace and please them all so no one would yell. As a result, I fluctuated between feeling invisible but wanting to be seen, and wishing I was *actually* invisible, so people wouldn't stare at me or make demands. I felt most comfortable in my room alone, hiding so I wouldn't have to deal with other people's needs. I remember many nights thinking before going to sleep, *it would be okay if I just never woke up.*

I also was a sickly kid and enjoyed the extra attention I received when I was ill. So, unconsciously, I learned that being a 'victim' got me the notice I craved, but was afraid to ask for. In addition, because I was so sensitive, my family was overly protective of me. All of this caused me to be very apprehensive of change of any kind. Any difference in the environment or routine was just too scary.

In grammar school, I was teased a lot because of my stuttering, but I slowly moved forward despite my fears, and as I became braver, my speech improved. By senior year of high school, the tics were gone, and I managed to eliminate (or hide) most of the stuttering, but I was still quite insecure and very overweight.

When I was fifteen, a friend fixed me up, and we went on a double date. After we arrived at the restaurant, my date spoke privately to his friend, then suggested he and I go for a ride alone. I was afraid to say no. He ended up driving me home and telling me he was sorry, but he couldn't possibly be seen with someone so overweight. I walked into the house, humiliated and crying, and never went on another high school date. Then I went on a drastic diet and took off all my extra weight before graduation. My brother got one of his handsome friends to take me to the senior prom, where I felt like Cinderella at the ball.

My friend Renie, the only one who called me Jan instead of Janis, went to UMASS with me. From then on, I was known as Jan. As a freshman in college, I found the stress of having so many boys wanting to take me out frightening since I had virtually NO dating experience, so I wound up gaining back all my weight. Hiding was still safer than taking risks. After graduation, I was hired in Boston as a computer programmer. I became good at it, and thought, *Thank God, I'm a programmer, because what else would I do?* I soon moved up the ranks and landed in New York City as a project manager.

Eventually, I met my husband-to-be, Shelly (a psychologist), at a singles event. I couldn't believe someone so handsome and bright wanted to date me, but he was several years younger than I was, so I kept pushing him away and saying I was too old for him. Thank goodness, he never listened.

Transitioning – Starting to Learn my Lessons

When we were dating, Shelly convinced me to try talk therapy as a way to get to know myself better. I was hesitant about marrying him because I worried I would lose myself and spend all my energy taking care of my husband.

I was successful at work, but at great expense to myself. I was the martyr at my company, always the last to leave the office, and sometimes bullied by bosses into working tons of overtime with no extra pay. However, I was fortunate to have an excellent therapist and slowly began to love and appreciate myself. What I found out from therapy was the first major shift in my life.

I realized that going after what I wanted was better than not even trying for fear of failing. I learned that I could (and should) speak up for myself, rather than doing what everyone else wanted me to do. I learned that even if I did fail, I had done the best I could, and I'd integrated lessons that made me stronger going forward. With my self-esteem restored and determined to take more risks, I finally felt safe enough to marry Shelly. He and I have now been happily married for over thirty-five years.

Soon, my career took off. I moved to the business area of Polygram Records (now Universal Music Group) and became vice president of the East Coast Royalty Accounting Department, which handled all royalties for such labels as Island, Def Jam, Verve, and more. I found the music business to be a tough environment, but also a fun industry. One of the more important things I learned here was to never let people push me around. Bullies do indeed back down when confronted with dignity and honesty. I felt I had made it in the business world while still maintaining my integrity and enjoying my work—plus I had a successful marriage.

What I still hadn't found was my passion.

Then, one weekend, this aspect of my life opened up. While I've since learned that the Universe (God, Source, whatever you want to call it) leads us where we need to be, at the time, I thought finding my calling was simply a coincidence.

My husband, who has for many years played basketball a few times a week, signed up for a weekend basketball camp at Omega Institute (a holistic retreat in upstate New York). Shelly then threw the catalog at me and said, "Pick a workshop and come along." So I looked through the listings and saw a picture of a wild-looking woman who was teaching a workshop called Energy Medicine. I had no idea what that was, but I registered for the class.

During the first day of the 'mostly girls' Donna Eden workshop, we were taught a routine to raise energy and also several ways to eliminate pain. When Shelly returned to our cabin at 5 pm and stood in the doorway, sweating and breathing hard, he said, "I'm so exhausted, I don't think I can even make it to the shower."

Suddenly, I sat up and said, "I CAN HELP YOU WITH THAT."

I then proceeded to show Shelly how to 'thump' on his lymphatic system to stir up energy, and in about two minutes, he announced, "*Wow*! That was *fantastic*. What did we just do?" before running into the shower.

That was it. I'D FOUND MY PASSION, and I was hooked.

When we returned home, I called a friend who was housebound with a pinched nerve in her back. I told her about my workshop and offered to try to help with her pain. She agreed, even though I explained I couldn't guarantee anything. After much time preparing to help her, I saw her the next day, and by the end of an hour, her pain was gone. We were both amazed. However, the next morning, I woke up with HER pain in MY leg. So I had to heal myself, but learned an important lesson: *Protect yourself* before you work with others.

Evolving

Since that first holistic workshop, I've learned so many things, and am so grateful.

I took more Donna Eden workshops, and eventually became a teaching assistant for Donna. In 2006, with her husband David's encouragement, I launched my own energy practice. When Donna formed a certification program, I graduated from her inaugural class, and I'm now a practitioner listed on her website.

I also became certified by Gary Craig, founder of Emotional Freedom Technique (some people call it 'tapping'). EFT is a type of energy psychology that helps with trauma, phobias, fears, and so much more, including physical ailments. I'm now an emotional assistant for Dawson Church at his NYC workshops, and a listed practitioner on Dawson's website, EFT Universe, where I've published two articles.

All this has led me to many other holistic certifications, and to becoming an interfaith minister. Energy medicine wasn't well known in 2006, and people didn't understand it. At energy conferences, colleagues recommended becoming an interfaith minister in order to have more "serious" credentials. They said, "Google the Universal Life Church and buy a certificate saying you're a minister." I knew that wouldn't work, because it wouldn't feel authentic to ME. This was also complicated by the fact that I was (and am) a practicing Jew. So I rejected the option of becoming a minister until I finally got the courage—or possibly push from the Universe—to look into interfaith ministries. That's how I found The New Seminary, an interfaith seminary with a two-year path to ordination.

I reviewed their curriculum: classes in different religions, and instruction in various rituals (baby naming, healing, marriages, funerals, leading services, etc.), and I thought, *I can do that*. I went to an open house and spoke to the deans in charge. I told them I was Jewish and was initially interested in the seminary to get more credentials for my energy work, but was honestly intrigued by their syllabus. I also confessed, "I may never function as a real minister." They smiled and said many people were unsure where ordination would lead them, and that was okay.

So I enrolled, and what followed were two of the most wonderful and important years of my life. The hidden agenda of The New Seminary turned out to be personal growth and learning to be present and getting the ego out of the way. This was my second huge shift.

Many of us came into the seminary as serial 'rescuers', who felt our job was to heal the world and take care of everyone we came into contact with. However, we learned in those two years that ministers don't heal anyone, and neither do energy practitioners or doctors or any other humans. Our job is to get out of our heads, and simply be present by listening to our clients. They're the ones with the answers. Our role is to use our gifts and tools to help them find the power and solutions within themselves.

By the way, I also now truly function as a minister, performing weddings, funerals, healing rituals, and such.

So by then, my life had turned 180 degrees from where I'd started out. I had spent years in therapy learning to shrink my superego—that judgmental voice inside myself—and grow my ego—my valid sense of self—so that I could learn to forgive myself, love myself, respect myself, and stand up for myself. That was critical to having a successful marriage, a wonderful business career, and so forth.

Now that I had all those positives, I had to incorporate understanding in some more subtle aspects of life in order to give back for all that I had received.

I came to realize that I needed to get myself out of the way and truly stand humbly beside others—not as a superior, or someone with all the answers, but just as a fellow human being. To move out of my head and away from my need to help or heal—and just BE. Be present, be nonjudgmental, listen, and use my knowledge and tools to show clients that they have the POWER and the ANSWERS inside themselves.

Where multitasking had been a critical asset to my business success, I now had to slow down and focus in order to be present and helpful in this one-on-one world of healing. Most importantly, I learned that a much higher power than Jan was in action in all of this. You can call it the Universe, or God, or Source, or whatever name you like, but my faith and trust in this higher power is what allows me to relax and trust I'll be led where I need to be.

Lessons Learned Along the Way

So, in this journey through life, what are the key points I've learned so far?

First and foremost is that "attitude is everything." In Bruce Lipton's book, *Biology of Belief*, he proves that nurture triumphs over nature. For example, if we have a genetic disposition toward developing a disease, our attitude and how we are nurtured can actually transform us at the DNA level.

Beliefs are very powerful. If we don't think it's possible to do something, it's unlikely we'll ever even try, but if we open up to the possibility of doing it, whatever it is, we will expand our horizons.

My brother, Barry, died in a car accident when he was forty-two, a tragedy for all of us. By then, I had strayed from Judaism to agnosticism, not believing in much. But since my brother had been president of his synagogue in Massachusetts, I decided to honor him by finding a synagogue in New York City and saying the mourners' prayer, called Kaddish, every week for a year. After several weeks of my attending the minion—the gathering of mourners—the leader asked if I wanted to lead a minion with him, and then the president of the Sisterhood asked if I wanted to be part of the Sisterhood Sabbath service. My husband and I eventually joined the synagogue, and I found my spirituality again and my path back to God.

So this tragedy ended up being a hidden blessing for me that has enhanced my life in many ways. Since then, every time I thought I was doing someone a favor, it ended up being a favor to me instead. Every mishap and setback in my life after that time has ended up being a gift that taught me an important lesson. All because my attitude and outlook on life had changed. I have an 'attitude of gratitude' and have learned to appreciate what I do have, rather than regretting what I don't have.

Equally important is to choose accountability rather than victimhood. As a child, I was stuck in the victim mindset of feeling sorry for myself and wanting others to feel sorry for me as well. That prevented me from doing so many things. Not until I changed my attitude was I able to use the power within me to be proactive in my life. Now, even if I do believe that I'm not the source of a negative situation, I have a choice where I go from there:

- I can do nothing, continue blaming others, and wallow in misery. That will attract people who will pity me and help me stay stuck in victim mode.

Or

- I can accept responsibility for my situation no matter who I think got me into it and change my attitude to look for ways to move forward in a positive manner.

I remember years ago being so relieved when I 'fell' into programming, because "what else could I possibly do?" Once I expanded my vision, I was able to forge ahead and become a vice president of a major record company, and at the age of sixty-one, found my true passion in my ministry and energy work. I now am flexible and know I can do anything I set my sights on.

Another important aspect of accountability is learning to forgive. In the past, I held onto righteous anger against people who had hurt me. I eventually learned that anger harms me more than the person I thought had offended me. Thinking about who is right or who is wrong, or if my anger/hurt is justified or not is a waste of time. It doesn't matter.

I also came to understand that the hardest person to forgive is yourself. We're taught as children to feel guilt and shame.

We are all human, so once we learn to forgive ourselves, forgiving others becomes easier. If we hold onto the anger, it's a burden that we carry, but if we just let go and move on, we lighten our load. If our anger is against another person, we don't have to love the other person or even have a relationship with them again. We can just move on.

That's the next important lesson: focusing on the past is only helpful if we revisit it to see what we learned or were supposed to learn from it. No more *coulda, woulda, shoulda*.

When I was younger, I often ruminated on how my life would be so much better if only I had done this or that. Even if that were true, thinking so doesn't change things, because the past is just that—THE PAST. If I become stuck in that mode nowadays, I give myself about ten minutes to wallow, and then I say, *Okay, here I am right now, and I have the power to change anything I don't like from this moment on,* so I check to see if I was supposed to learn or re-learn something (because sometimes I do forget and fall into old traps). If I find a lesson, I apply it going forward. If not, then I release the past and just move on. If I mess up today, I always have tomorrow to correct myself again.

Another set of lessons that I learned has to do with my archetypes of 'rescuer', 'martyr', 'co-dependent', and the like.

As I said, growing up, I felt my job was to make situations better for everyone, keep the peace, heal people, and do what everyone else wanted—without regard for what I wanted or needed. In fact, many times, I rushed to help people who didn't want my help, and they were actually angry at me for interfering. This totally confounded me and made me angry that they didn't appreciate my sacrifice.

My time in the seminary really helped me learn to set boundaries, while dealing with some really ill people taught me the importance of stepping back, taking care of myself first, and not overstepping. As they say on the airplane, "Put on your own oxygen mask first. You can't help others before you help yourself."

I also learned that the height of conceit was to think that my job was to heal everyone else, and that I needed to have all the answers. That was exhausting. Even if someone did want my help, maybe helping them would just keep THEM in their victim mode.

I learned just being present and using my gifts and tools to help others find their own answers is really much better. Once they find their power and learn to be accountable for their own healing, it's a win-win for everyone.

One more important lesson was to **choose supportive people in your life**. In the past, when I refused to accept any positive feelings about myself, my negativity attracted a lot of negative people. Once I became flexible enough to open up to all my possibilities, I started attracting people who supported me and learned to let go of negative relationships. My husband, Shelly, has been a strong supportive force in my life, and my sister, Wendy, is also a constant who encourages me. I've attracted wonderful mentors in my business career, and wonderful colleagues and friends in my personal life. I feel very blessed to have so many people in my life who support me and who I can, in turn, support.

Finally, I learned not to try so hard to control everything, and to trust in a higher power. In addition to being a practicing Jew, I also belong to a non-denominational organization, where we simply surrender to God. In my view, being part of an organized religion doesn't matter, as long as we believe in something greater than ourselves, and have some place or way to access that higher power and know we're not alone. Often, I just find a quiet space and surrender to that power. I've learned that being humble, being authentic, and letting a higher power help me in my journey has made all the difference in allowing myself to grow and learn.

Now that I've gone from resisting change to acceptance of what life has to bring, I can't wait to see what new possibilities are waiting for me going forward, in this amazing phenomenon we call life.

Anza Goodbar

Anza Goodbar's giftedness is influencing people to identify their passion and reach their full potential. Her profound interest in understanding what causes people to feel worthy, visible and fulfilled gave her strength to face life's challenges head-on. Through intensive training and education, she has discovered how to love herself unconditionally, remove the shame of sexual and physical abuse from her story, and inspire others by rising above her circumstances.

She currently empowers her clients to overcome their fears and create deeper more intimate relationships from the boardroom to the bedroom through private coaching, mastermind groups, public speaking, and couples' retreats.

Find Anza online:

www.anzagoodbar.com
www.instagram.com/anzagoodbar
www.facebook.com/coachanzagoodbar

Stepping into Freedom

By Anza Goodbar

Have you ever felt like an ugly duckling? I have. When I was growing up, I was never thin enough to be considered beautiful. I recall my dad saying, "You'd be a beautiful creature if you'd just lose ten pounds."

It was always "just" ten more pounds to achieve his elusive ideal of beauty. No matter how small I became, I could never quite reach that goal. I felt like I was playing target practice with a blindfold on. Just when I thought I had reached the goal—the target would move.

Growing up, there was a great emphasis on physical beauty. Looking put together was far more important than feeling like you had it all together. My dad said, "With beauty comes great responsibility." I was never sure I was capable of handling that responsibility because I didn't feel beautiful on the inside.

You see, my mom's boyfriend started sexually molesting me when I was nine years old. He disguised it by playing tickle games and rolling around on the floor with me. It was an easy way to camouflage where his hands were going. I would scream for him to stop, but my mom thought it was all in good fun. It was just a game, after all.

There were times when he would come to our house for dinner or to just hang out. I'd fake being sick and force my mom to take me to the emergency room to avoid being near him. There was only a one in ten chance that would work, but I'd give it my best effort, and sometimes I'd get lucky.

Several months later, my mother and her boyfriend announced they were getting married. I was devastated; my world felt like it was coming to an end. How could she choose him over me? How could she not see what he was doing to me right under her nose?

I locked myself in the car and refused to come out. This was, of course, long before there were cell phones, so I had to wait to use his phone to call my dad. I had always been a compliant kid, so I thought this act of outright defiance would flip a switch and make the light come on.

We didn't have a home phone, so the next time we went to his house, I called my dad. Little did I know that my mom was listening in on the phone in the kitchen. I pleaded with him to not make me go to the wedding. I begged him to let me come and live with him.

He was hesitant. After the divorce, he had two male roommates, and he wasn't sure it would be the right environment to raise a little girl. My tears and sobbing finally convinced him it was worth a try. My mother told him that I was just playing house, and I'd be back home with her and her new husband in a week. I lived with my dad from that time forward. I never returned home full-time with my mom.

Shortly after the wedding, they moved out of town, so I didn't have to see them often. On visits, given the opportunity, he would sneak inappropriate touches.

As I grew older and learned how to drive, I had more freedom to be out of the house during his waking hours. He worked at a mine, so shift work was part of his routine. I'd schedule my visits to minimize my exposure to him. I'd invite a friend to drive up with me for the weekend to thwart any opportunity that he might find to corner me.

As I was growing up, my parents anticipated that I'd be sexually active before marriage. They encouraged me to tell them when I felt I was going to be ready, so I could be put on birth control. As I look back, it's no wonder that I became pregnant at sixteen.

Just before we discovered my pregnancy, my dad sent me to live with my mom and stepdad to get me away from my boyfriend. He was several years older than I was, so my dad didn't approve of our relationship.

On the three-and-a-half-hour drive to my mom's house, I started to feel sick. I grabbed a Sprite on the way out the door for the trip, and I began to sip it to settle my stomach. By the time we arrived, I was full-on vomiting. I thought I had the flu that was going around school, but my mother knew better. At her first sight of me, she knew I was pregnant. She set up an appointment to see the doctor the following day to confirm her suspicion.

As if that wasn't enough to deal with, my dad said if I wanted to live with him, I'd have to abort the baby. When I told him that an abortion wasn't an option for me, he asked, "Where will you live?" My heart sank. The promises of "always being here no matter what" evaporated right before my eyes. All I could sadly muster up was, "I guess not at home with you."

My mom's response to my situation was, "You made your bed, now you get to sleep in it!" Not very helpful. She was angry because I had gone off the pill when the doctor I was seeing told me I was sterile, based on some female trouble I had been having.

With one choice, my life was forever changed. The way people viewed me was different. All of a sudden, I was stupid. My potential had somehow vanished. No one in my family could see any hope for my future beyond welfare and poverty. College was certainly out of the picture.

Reality set in quickly. I had limited choices in my current situation. I could stay with my mom and stepdad and hide my pregnancy in order to finish the school year, or I could marry my high school sweetheart and complete high school in my hometown.

At sixteen, I thought I knew what love was, and that I could figure things out. I had this happily-ever-after story all mapped out. We'd just move our plans up a few years, and everything would work out as we had planned, albeit a few years ahead of schedule.

I stayed at my mother's house for a couple of weeks while we prepared to get married and move into our first apartment. The night before my boyfriend was coming to pick me up, I was home alone with my stepdad packing up for the move. As I was boxing up my belongings in my bedroom, he flung the door open. His enormous presence filled the doorway with his 5'10' frame.

He was a sturdy man weighing nearly 400 pounds. He pushed me onto the bed. My heart was racing. I was trying to hold back tears and hide the terror that was bubbling up in my throat. He leaned over me, and I could feel the weight of his chest pinning me to the bed. It was hard to breathe. He leaned closer and whispered in my ear, "What would you do if I raped you tonight?"

I must have looked like a frightened kitten to him. His eyes mocked me as he said, "Go ahead and scream. There's no one around to hear you." Then he released my wrists and walked out of the room laughing.

I could smell his cologne. It gagged me as I choked back tears. I was trembling. He felt like he owned me. I was nothing more than a plaything in his sick game of cat and mouse. I could hardly wait for morning to come so I could leave and finally feel safe.

The power he held over me would reduce me to a frightened child, even into adulthood. For years, I stayed away from my family because of the horror of being in his presence. My kids always wondered why we didn't go to Grandma's house very often. I would play it off as the trip was too far to make on a weekend, or we were too busy to make the drive.

It took colossal amounts of mental preparation and energy when we would go to visit. I would meticulously plan every detail from the time we arrived until the time we left. I always orchestrated having someone in the room with me, so he couldn't touch me. Nevertheless, he always managed to nudge past the people in the room to rub up next to me, pretending it was an accident.

I was thankful my mom didn't like to travel, so I never had to worry about him invading my home. That all changed the summer I was going through a divorce from my second husband. After more than a decade of emotional abuse, going to counseling and still not being able to create a healthy relationship, I was ready to stand on my own two feet. I was done feeling like a second-class citizen in my own home.

With my sights set firmly on starting fresh, my parents decided it would be a great idea to come and support me. I tried to say no. I used every excuse I could think of to get out of it, to no avail. They had made up their minds that they were coming.

I felt like a trapped animal. The closer it came to them arriving, the more fear gripped my soul. Had I actually *been* a trapped animal, I would have chewed my leg off to escape. I was in an emotional frenzy. I could barely contain my fear. My breath came in short, shallow gasps. My senses were on full alert.

When they arrived, I was in my tiny U-shaped kitchen—barely large enough for one person. While my mom went to the restroom, my stepdad blocked the entry, arms fully extended touching the refrigerator and the wall, so I couldn't escape. I panicked. My emotions were raw, and I was scared. The dirty secret I tried to keep from my kids was about to explode like hot lava spewing from a volcano.

I tried to back away, but he kept advancing toward me. My back was up against the counter. He reached out and brushed his hand along the side of my right breast. That was it! I couldn't hold it in. I was hysterical! I started sobbing and screaming, "Get out of my house! Don't touch me! Get out of my house! Don't touch me!"

My mom came running out of the restroom, unable to grasp what she was hearing. She was confused, hurt, and trying to understand why I was so out of my mind with hysteria. She kept assuring me that "they were just here to support me." She repeatedly asked me, "Why are you so upset?" All I could utter was, "Get out, just get *out.*"

My kids were mortified by my behavior. They had never seen me react in such an out of control, emotional way. I had to come clean and share with them what had happened to me repeatedly as a child, and the terror I felt in his presence.

We didn't speak for months at a time. I was not equipped to deal with the feelings that followed the eruption. All the emotions I kept safely tucked away were all on the surface. There was no denying them or ignoring them. I didn't know where to start healing.

Over the years, I tried to talk to my mom about it, but she could never admit that she knew. Her inability to acknowledge what had happened made me feel like she didn't care, or that she didn't want me. What I have come to understand is that if she were to admit she was aware of his vile actions, the man she believed him to be when she married him was a falsehood. That would have changed her reality. That would have meant her marriage was built on a lie.

As I look back on my life, those abusive events created a love/hate relationship with food. On the one hand, food brought me great comfort, but on the other hand, it was a shameful escape. Weight became a constant rollercoaster of putting on extra pounds. I could lose the weight, but I could never keep it off. It affected my confidence and my belief that I was worthy or deserving of love.

I longed to be beautiful on the inside, but I always felt dirty and less-than. I felt expendable because no one listened to my cries for help. Years later, I had aunts and uncles admit they knew something was going on, but they didn't feel it was their place to interfere.

Internally I cried out...when is it not the time to protect a child? When is it not the time to stand up for those who don't have a voice? Why was I expendable? Why wasn't I valuable enough to stand up for? What was lacking in me? I grappled with those questions for years.

Because of those experiences, I always felt like I had to work harder, to be more, to be perfect. Perfection was the standard I thought I had to achieve to be loved, to be valued, to be redeemable. This belief system permeated my personal and professional life.

Perfection and people pleasing go hand in hand. They lead you down a path that undermines your identity at the core level. I lost sight of who I was in my very being. I believed that I wasn't enough as I was, so I put on masks and performed to attain love, affection, and approval. These behaviors are the killers of self-esteem, self-compassion, and self-love. I began to believe the lie that I didn't deserve love, affection or that happily-ever-after, storybook ending.

Shame made me feel isolated and set apart. Every aspect of my life was filled with shame, and it began to rule my thinking. I became invisible. I didn't want my secrets to define me; yet for years, they did. I feared that people would judge me, so I shied away from friendships and being a part of a community. I denied myself the most basic of human needs...to be known.

As a young woman, I didn't understand that shame couldn't survive in the presence of compassion. I didn't have a trusted support system to confide in. For decades, I hid my shame as it ate away at me. I knew that there had to be more to life than what I had experienced, but I didn't have a clear path to get there.

I knew I wanted to inspire women with my story, but my story wasn't complete, and I didn't feel like I had a voice to tell it. I didn't believe that people would listen. I was a hidden face of nameless women who had experienced similar stories. #MeToo

Then, I began to ponder, *Who will speak for those who don't have the courage to speak for themselves? Who will help them feel visible and seen?* I didn't have an answer to those questions until a friend asked me, "If not you...then who? If not now...then when?"

I was terrified to share my story after so many years of trying to keep it buried. The secrets I held close to my heart would expose me as being frail and weak. I didn't want to be seen as a victim. I didn't want those words to define me.

I have worked hard to get past those dark days and create a life where I feel whole, and where I can honestly say I love myself unconditionally. I have intentionally forgiven the people in my life who failed to protect me and, thankfully, I have restored my relationship with my mom.

The past couple of years have been a season of new awareness, growth, and healing for me. I have discovered that I had a pattern of using weight as a coping mechanism when I feel threatened. While journaling about my relationship with food and exercise, I began to connect the dots between food and abuse. Every major weight gain was the result of feeling violated by an inappropriate encounter with a man. Immediately I ran to food for comfort. Food was something I could control. Subconsciously, I believed if I was overweight, I'd be less desirable. I'd be safe.

It was a vicious cycle. Food provided temporary comfort, but it also induced guilt and shame stemming from my inability to stand up for myself. I knew I should be able to speak up for myself, but the experience of being violated made me feel small and insignificant. My throat would get tight and rendering me unable to utter a sound. I felt small and powerless.

This topic came up in a conversation with my coach as we were discussing my resistance to raising my visibility in my business. I hated the body I saw in the mirror every day. It wasn't the one I saw in my mind. It wasn't a body I wanted others to see. I didn't fit my dad's idea of beauty. It was all starting to make sense.

She challenged me to pen a love letter to my body. It was one of the most difficult letters I ever tried to write. She instructed me to leave out the negative language I'd been using to describe myself and my body and encouraged me to replace that verbiage with gratitude and appreciation for my entire being. She asked me to dedicate a portion of the letter to asking for forgiveness for the times I had abused my body by not eating right or exercising to take care of it. It was disarming, humbling, and empowering at the same time.

At the time, I was part of a mastermind group. My coach challenged me to be courageous and share my letter with our private Facebook group. That was one of the most vulnerable steps in my healing journey. I sat for hours staring at my computer screen. *Should I or shouldn't I share my letter? Will be judged by the women in the group? What value could there be for me? Will the other women even relate to my struggle?*

After copying and pasting my words, then deleting them for the umpteenth time, I finally said, "Go big or go home!" I clicked the post button and walked away. The fear of what might happen became smaller than the curiosity of what I might learn to from the experience. The responses I received were filled with overwhelming love and support. My coach said she wept publicly on the bus as she read my letter. It was then that I knew my life mattered and that I could have an impact.

As I have shared my experience on other platforms, it has given others the courage to tell their story and suffocate their shame in compassion. It opened up a safe space for them to share their struggles with body image, self-love, and self-esteem and set them on a path to transform their lives from tragedy to triumph.

How do we become whole again and find our personal power?

- By telling our truth is how we get our power back.
- By shouting from the rooftops until someone hears us and believes our story is how we get our power back.
- By standing boldly, looking into our mirrors naked, and being unashamed of our bodies is how we get our power back.

How do we acknowledge that abuse is never our fault, and how do we take our power back?

- By acknowledging that it was someone else's job to protect us and they let us down is how we take our power back.

- By recognizing that our abusers gained power by making others feel small is how we take our power back.

Today, I can share my story without attributing blame or feeling shame. I can tell it without emotion or assigning a value of the good or bad. They were events that happened in my past, but they no longer define who I am.

The fact that I was resilient and never gave up is what defines who I am. I am an overcomer. I am a survivor. I am the hero in my own story.

The biggest lesson I have learned from sharing my story is that I have a powerful voice. I can inspire women and men alike. I can influence people regardless of race, generation, or affluence.

Everyone loves to root for the underdog, and today they get to hear that happily-ever-after ending! I was that underdog. I was the girl everyone wrote off. Today, I have a voice that can invoke transformation into the lives of others because I have learned how to love and accept myself and my story unconditionally. And, through that journey, I have created a wildly happy life.

I am the mother of four amazing adult kids and one adorable granddaughter. I was their biggest advocate. I held space for them in ways my parents didn't for me. Yes, there was a cost, but it was a cost worth paying. I now have the self-respect and confidence that I could only dream of as a child.

Because of these experiences, I have committed my life to helping one million women transform their lives by teaching them how to love themselves unconditionally. By helping them develop self-care strategies. By showing them how to revise their self-talk, become more self-compassionate and, most importantly, by improving their body image and redefining beauty so they can feel empowered from the boardroom to the bedroom.

This is your time. Live your life out loud. Own your story. Be proud of the journey you've taken. It's never too late to rewrite your ending!

This is your life. You get to define what beauty and success mean to you. You don't have to be limited by how others see you or judge you. In fact, I tell myself it's none of my business what others think of me. It's my business to be better tomorrow than I am today.

I hope you will dare to be the woman or man you know you were created to be!

Suzanne LaVoie

Suzanne LaVoie is a seasoned writer filled with a huge zest for her craft and life. Her literary achievements include being a contributing chapter author for two compilations, including *Unsung Heroes: Deconstructing Suicide through Stories of Triumph* and *What's Self-Love Got to Do With It?* Suzanne is also a solo author and launched her first book of a series, *Knight Shift*, in December 2017.

Suzanne obtained a Master's in Social Work with a concentration in international and community development from Monmouth University. She has been a public speaker at various venues and performs with a drama group that educates about diverse mental health topics. Suzanne has a love for travel and currently works as an author liaison, content editor and proofreader for Follow It Thru Publishing, a writing coach for Your Shift Matters Publishing, and as an online trainer for Ashley Consulting and Training.

Find Suzanne online:

www.suzannelavoiewrites.com
https://www.linkedin.com/in/suzanne-lavoie-sammon-a0981162
https://m.facebook.com/coolwritersuzanne

Open Up the Airways of Your Life

By Suzanne LaVoie

My life journey, path, or whatever term someone wants to use, has been "circuitous." My beloved mother was the first person to describe it this way. I used other vocabulary many times to express how I felt about the never-ending twists, turns, bumps, falls, rejections, disappointments throughout my existence, but she was (and still is) my biggest encourager and cheerleader. We had a conversation a few months ago where she stated that I was born brave. This statement arose from a chronic health issue that I will expand on in this chapter. Truthfully, I never really saw it this way until she stated it. I always associated bravery with someone running into a burning building and rescuing people and their pets. I admired the superheroes of my time and wished day after day for those mighty powers that would allow them to fly, jump over bridges, and lift up items that weighed tons. Truth be known, I was also drawn to how revered these 'brave' souls were by other people. I craved that in my own life.

"I am sorry to have to say this to you both, but your daughter only has a 50/50 chance of survival."

This was stated to both of my parents in the hospital emergency room in the middle of the night by the attending pediatrician. I was only three years old at the time. A couple of days previously, I was sick with a regular common cold. Then I was literally at death's door.

I never had children, but I can only begin to imagine what was going through my parents' minds at that moment. I now know from conversations years later, which revealed that my mother and father blamed themselves because they didn't get me to the hospital sooner. Helplessness and fear were overwhelming. Here was a doctor who wasn't even my regular pediatrician having to break some of the worst news to two strangers—that their daughter was possibly going to die that night. I get chills as I think and write about it. I would not wish that kind of agony on anyone. In the meantime, I was in another part of the hospital gasping for any breath that I could take, wheezing and coughing like mad. I remember there were staff workers everywhere trying to save my life and helping me to just breathe.

Life can be suffocating at times. Unexpected news, a health issue, or a relationship ending can feel like someone literally stuffed a pillow over our face. We can't see or suck in the air we need for proper oxygen intake. Panic sets in. We fight and struggle against what is blocking our senses. I have been there many times. I sometimes believe that part of the reason I was born with this chronic condition was to understand more in the figurative sense of how obstacles can stifle our dreams, goals, and purposes. Unfortunately, sometimes it is the people closest to us who can become those pillows. I think about how furniture in our homes are covered with pillows and other linens. While two or three are sufficient enough, there can be overkill with it, and the natural beauty of the couch or chair is drowned out. Sometimes we can even be our own worst pillows.

Getting back to the emergency room—the pediatrician who was on call that night was the best in his profession. Obviously, the fact that this chapter is being written is proof of that (I am alive and well to compose it!). However, as part of my recovery, I spent days and days in an oxygen tent. A lot of my younger peers have no idea that they even existed when I mention it. My parents could view me from outside of the tent, but they could not touch me. I wasn't even allowed to watch TV because back then there was fear that a spark from the television could mix with the oxygen and KABOOM! Interestingly enough, I did receive a spark during that time; it was the igniting of my creative juices, my imagination, that part of my mind where ideas and scenarios were conceived. My parents were told by the nurses and other workers that I seemed to occupy my time in the tent wonderfully, and never complained. Back then, they had these stickers that were designed to look like medals, and at the bottom of the sticker was the word BRAVE. I received a number of them throughout my various hospital stays. I probably had enough to achieve a high military rank, were they the real deal. The sad truth is I forgot about these medals. I never thought about them again until the conversation with my mother regarding my being born brave. I should have stuck them all over my room and then taken them with me when I moved on. Too many pillows were stuffed over my face, and I was blinded.

Today there is a compelling amount of awareness to do with asthma, but that was not the case when I was going to school. In fact, I was often chastised as wanting attention; therefore, I was making it up when an attack came on. Now, let's get real here. Yes, kids do crave attention and will sometimes engage in acts that bring on that absorption from the adults in their lives; however, to look at a child who is practically turning blue and crying from harsh inhaling, and believe she/he is making it up? I specifically remember a time when I collapsed on the school playground, and one of my classmates ran inside to get help. The nurse came out with a wheelchair along with one of the principals. There I was, half-lying on the dirty pavement wheezing, and the assistant principal towered over me with a scowl stating that if I was making this up, I was going to be in a lot of trouble. Sure, just add some gasoline to the fire! I didn't realize until my later childhood years that stress and fear brought on a lot of asthmatic attacks, and I had a lot of reasons to feel this way. It wasn't bad enough that I was in physical agony, on display in front of all the kids on the playground; now, I was once again being accused of being theatrical with a threat of retribution!

Through my personal journey of self-discovery, I have come to accept that back then those authority figures were acting out of their own lack of knowledge, and I can't fully blame them for that. They did, however, have a choice to be compassionate, which was sorely lacking at that time. They could have sat down with me, tried to comfort me, anything that could have helped calm me down—nope, that was not the case. If anything, I was treated as a burden and a headache.

When I was released from my hospital stays, I often had to stay at home for a few more days to recover. I loved my coloring books, my Colorforms, and my kiddie stories. I would read the same books over and over again to the point where I could recite the pages myself. I began to do this when I played on my swing set and even to some of the kids at school. It was one of the few precious times that I received positive feedback from my peers when I recounted the stories with no notes. I also developed an obsession with notebook paper. I believe in my heart that it was the beginning of my passion for writing. There was a particular kind of paper in the classroom that I really admired, and I would help myself to tons of it (yes, I am making a confession here). I loved the deep blue lines and the smoothness of it.

Additionally, my mom introduced me to a purple pen which, back then, was a rare gem. I would proudly show my classwork around with my newfound ink color. Well, I became the envy of every student around me, and some even begged to use it for their own assignments. I used this pen any time I wrote, and the joy it brought me and others was priceless. Writing became my saving grace.

Throughout my adolescent and college years, I was still dealing with asthma, plus an amalgam of other health challenges, both physical and mental. I was put on a slew of medications, especially for depression, anxiety, and post-traumatic stress disorder. While the medications helped with some of the critical issues, a mammoth side effect was weight gain. Mind you, when I was hospitalized for asthma, I was often on steroidal interventions (my body has stretch marks to this day from the side effects); in those days, it was the only way to properly and adequately resolve my breathing difficulties. In the later years, I was put on inhalers. I kept gaining weight, and this is was what my reality showcased:

"You're making this up."

"You're just depressed."

"Other people have it worse than you."

"It's all in your head."

"You're looking for attention."

"You just need to lose weight. Then you'll be fine."

All of my life. This is what I heard and was exposed to throughout the various stages of my journey. Fiery, emotional arrows that seared into the depths of my mental and spiritual well-being. They surely began from the earliest recollections of childhood, the years where my mind and brain were like a sponge; soaking in every single verbal lashing provided to me by those who were in positions to do the exact opposite. No empowerment; no encouragement; no belief in me or my gifts. My mind and spirit became a barren, charred land crying out to be watered and nurtured.

Between the years of 2011 through 2017, I was besieged by a barrage of additional health crises, and I sought help anywhere I could. The earlier quotes rang in my head, and each doctor I begged to take everything seriously was met with resistance. To them, I was an overweight, lazy, undisciplined, whiny female who just had to stop eating and get over myself. Yes, I admit I often used food as a means of coping with the crazy, chaotic hurricane of circumstances surrounding me, but I knew— KNEW—that there was something else going on. I prayed to God that someone would at least listen.

By the year 2016, I was experiencing some very intense symptoms. To put it in a nutshell, I was living in the bathroom, and the toilet became my new best friend. I was dealing with unbelievable gastrointestinal issues that would not let up. By 2017, I was practically housebound. However, it was at this time that a shift, a *monumental* shift, took root in my life. It was what I had been praying for, something new to enter the parched land of my body and soul.

Years prior, I had a goal—a very special goal—to write a book. As referenced earlier, I loved books and reading in general. Writing was a byproduct of that affection. I had a dream of holding a publication in my own hands that had my name under the title — something that was created with passion, emotion, yearning, and devotion. I reflected on how the act of writing a book was akin to a painter with his/her sketchpad, canvas, etc. That tangible result was birthed by you and only you and would become a legacy to loved ones and so many more. That goal was screaming to come out but was being suffocated by sabotaging thoughts and actions. The shift had its own power and was in this tug-of-war with the darkness and hopelessness that reigned in my life. Thank God that the shift ultimately won. The power of faith led me to victory. During 2016 and 2017, the goal manifested. I became a published author! I remember the day I held my first book. I treasure that moment and will always remember it.

Life, however, was not easy at all during this time, not by a longshot. Truthfully, during 2017, I was faced with my most frightening symptom yet. As someone who had a reputation for an excellent memory, almost photographic, the following symptom was the worst to confront; I was chronically forgetful. I would be sitting at my laptop writing and forget what I was working on. I would be driving on a route that I knew like the back of my hand and forget where I was. I would forget who someone was, or their name. After having lost my grandmother to dementia, the horror that I could possibly be experiencing this at such an early age was too much to bear. I struggled with suicidal thoughts, which wasn't the only time in my life where that occurred. Losing my mind was something I didn't know how to handle or cope with. I needed help. I needed answers!

I reached out to a former doctor of mine, and I was body-shamed once again. That was it! I was done with the narrow-mindedness and tunnel vision of some of the medical staff I encountered and advocated for someone who would listen and do the right thing. Well, it FINALLY happened. After being told that I had no issues (it was just weight-related), I was led to the most amazing specialist who actually took everything to heart and didn't stop until she uncovered the truth. I was diagnosed with a pre-cancerous condition that needs to be monitored, but then in April of this year, I was diagnosed with SIBO (small intestine bacterial overgrowth). SIBO was the answer to SO many issues that I have been dealing with for years! It took one person to listen, gain the information, process it all, and think outside the box. One of the colossal reasons I was so bloated and gaining weight was due to my body retaining hydrogen from all of the bacteria in my system. In fact, my doctor diagnosed SIBO through a breathing test. When she initially explained to me that I had to go through a breathing test to determine the diagnosis, I thought to myself, *A breathing test? Don't you have the wrong end?* She then informed me that the test measures the level of gas in your system—it could be hydrogen or methane. Sure enough, I was loaded with hydrogen. All I was thinking was, thank God no one lit a match around me! Or that I didn't float away!

I finally had my answer. I really did have something wrong. I wasn't making it up. It wasn't in my head. I wasn't saying these things to get attention. I couldn't just lose the weight. I couldn't just get over it! I knew there was something there all along. I could have given in to all of the mammoth resistance that I was up against, but I stayed the course. I pushed against it. Heck, I slammed against it! The shift happened.

We all have shifts in our lives. We don't always understand why certain things happen. We had so many plans; yet, illness, a divorce, or car accident could totally throw our lives into unexpected chaos, and we are sitting there wondering *what now?*

I am here to tell and encourage you that life—though it won't be the same—can be different, and sometimes, even better than we could have imagined. We all have that power inside of us to make a choice—will we resist the shift and keep hanging onto what was, or we will embrace it with resilience and allow the shift to bring something new into our lives?

I made the decision to move forward, and today I am feeling so much better. Unfortunately, SIBO is something I will be living with the rest of my life, but the good news is, it can be managed. I never knew how certain foods were contributing to the bacteria, and that included some 'healthy' foods. It's a lot of trial and error, but I am enjoying my new journey. Food was a coping mechanism for me for a long time; now it is fuel for me to enjoy my best life. I have shared a lot about SIBO with others in my circle, and now others are getting tested for it as well. I suffered needlessly for years with these symptoms, and I don't want anyone else to go through it. Even my asthma has improved.

During some of the most gut-wrenching trials of my life, there have been multiple times where I asked God why He kept me alive that night when I had a 50/50 chance of survival. I was angry at times that He did save me because I felt that I had no purpose. I didn't understand how anything that happened could be used for good. I didn't even believe that God loved me. I used to refer to myself as God's mistake. But the last two years have revealed to me that God had a purpose in mind all along. He sought to turn around everything on my path that was meant to harm me. But I had to be the one to make the initial change. I had to shift my thinking.

Let's get back to the pillow analogy I discussed early on in the chapter. How many times do we cover our true beauty, talents, and abilities with the pillows of lies, fear, anger, control, and despair? How about the opinions of others? Eventually, the life gets sucked out of us because we are completely overpowered by all of these external obstructions. When I couldn't breathe during an asthmatic attack, it was due to a blockage in my airways. I required the correct medicine to penetrate the blockage and reopen the airway, so that I could breathe normally again. How about the internal blockages in our mind, body, and soul? There are so many we allow to set up camp inside, and then we are in trouble. It's like old food that is left in your refrigerator. Eventually, it begins to smell horrible, and even if your fridge is stocked with everything else fresh, the smell from the spoiled food will overpower everything. Nothing will look appetizing at that point because all that is around you is that horrendous odor. If you remove the old and put it where it belongs, then the new is free to be. Such as with us.

When we believe lies, endure abuse, stay in toxic relationships and situations, or allow opinions of others to rule us, our lives become like one huge asthmatic attack. We can't breathe, and we can't live to our fullest potential. We need to embrace the shift to go from resistance to resilience, and then to rebuilding. I am living a life today that is beyond anything that I could have ever imagined for myself. By the end of 2018, I will have published two solo books and three compilations, including this one. This is a long way from the little girl who was stuck in an oxygen tent. Being practically homebound forced me to see the calling placed upon my life. Now I say to God all of the time that I am grateful He saved me that night. Would I want to experience all that I went through again? Heck, no! But it was all part of the woman who is here today to speak her truth, claim her power, and share her passion with the world. I am brave.

This chapter was written to inspire and empower. My life has been deluged with many wounds, more than I care to count. This is not the end of the story, however. From these gashes sprang new paths, perspectives, growth, and inner power. My faith in God increased in immeasurable ways. This chapter is about my personal mission statement. It contains hope and vision bred by pain and tribulation. It is my story of shifting from a place of darkness to a universe of light. It is my gift to share with the world.

What about your gifts? What about your messages, testimonies, and stories of hope? They are all there, just waiting to be discovered. Just as an archaeologist digs deep for hidden treasures, so it is with you—dig down deep inside of you and know, *really know*, that there are precious diamonds within that are meant to come to light. Don't resist them; allow your resilience to shine

Stefanie Davis Miller

A dynamic female paramedic from Ontario Canada, Stefanie was a victim in the storm of the century (1993 in Florida), helping to save her sister and losing her best friend in a car accident on the same night. Two months later, she was sexually assaulted and developed PTSD at the age of seventeen. She remained undiagnosed for seven years until 2000.

Stefanie battled through a tough life that involved divorce and led to two beautiful children. She found a career in paramedicine as a way to give back. Stefanie now shares her story of resilience with others through international motivational speaking, writing and advocacy work for first responder mental health awareness through her organization called, Stefanie Speaks.

Find Stefanie online:

www.StefanieSpeaks.com
https://www.facebook.com/Stefanie.E.speaks/
https://www.linkedin.com/in/stefanie-miller-1b1546110/

My Light in the Darkness

By Stefanie Davis Miller

Some people are born with strength. Do you believe that? I'm not sure if I do. I have never seen myself as a strong person. Historically, I considered myself a follower. A far quieter, weaker individual in a group. I have forever been concerned with what others thought. Today, that can become a handicap for me if I'm not careful. I'm now told that I'm a very brave, strong person. People admire my strength, my resilience, and my courage. Was the strength always there? Thankfully, when the tough times arrived, my resilience kicked into high gear and got me through some of the most difficult experiences in my life.

My inner warrior has always been present, sitting quietly in the background, observing what is going on. She is cautious and doesn't feel the need to show herself all the time. You see, a true warrior is humble and functions to serve and protect others. She will show herself when necessary to advocate when needed, but often stays out of site. My warrior has experienced many, many battles over the years, from which she has been wounded. Some of those wounds have left scars. One of those scars is the self-belief that she is not worthy enough to stand up for herself. That is something she has been working on, and she is stronger today. She has been, without thought, always able to advocate for the vulnerable. This was true on the playground when she stood up for her little sister who was being bullied, and when she grabbed her sister years later during a very powerful tropical storm and dragged her to safety, when she put herself in harm's way to protect a friend and get her home safely.

The warrior grew even more with the birth of my two children. Mess with me, I may stay quiet; mess with my friends, my kids, someone who can't protect themselves—look out! The strength has always been there. I often need to be provoked in order to let my warrior out.

I have been forced to develop my resilience after exposure to a number of adverse events. I have had to grow and learn along my journey with many failures and many celebrated successes. My definition of strength *is* resilience. Strength shows up when you are scared to death. You don't want to move forward, but you ignore the fear. You ignore the fact that every fiber in your being is telling you to run. You put one foot in front of the other and move forward, because it is the right thing to do.

I became a paramedic ten years ago. I always felt the calling to help others and advocate for the vulnerable. The choice to become a paramedic was a no-brainer.

I quickly learned first-hand about the lack of support for those in the profession who come face to face with a mental health injury. Growing up, my dad was a police officer. Over the years, I observed that he was the 'go to' guy for fellow officers who needed to talk. Quiet conversations behind closed doors, officers showing up at our house while on shift, to talk. I would quietly watch the brief look of concern cloud my father's face. Dad sometimes spoke about officers who were alcoholics, whose serial marriages ended in divorce, the domestics, the suicides, even a couple of murder-suicides. As a teenager and young adult, I was somewhat aware there was a problem, a darkness, but didn't understand what it was or why, until I too became a first responder.

I had married in my early twenties. Shortly after we married, my first husband became a police officer. The darkness I had observed lurking around my dad, and the profession became my reality. The 180-degree change in personality, the behaviors, home visits by uniformed sergeants, angry outbursts, and the unrelenting depression. I can remember feeling so terribly sad, alone and afraid as the spouse of a police officer. I felt that no one understood what I was experiencing. I couldn't bring myself to talk to my parents. I felt isolated, confused, hurt, and ashamed. I used to tell myself I was the loneliest married person.

While searching online for support groups, I stumbled upon one for spouses of police officers. I felt hopeful. Perhaps this was part of the answer to my situation. One night, during an online chat, I jokingly referred to my husband as the Five-O (a police officer TV show). I guess the others in this help group didn't like that, as I sadly found myself suddenly blocked from communicating with them, without an explanation. As quickly as I had become a part of this support group, I was thrown out. I was devastated. I begged to be allowed back into the group to no avail, as this left me feeling more isolated than ever. My marriage continued to deteriorate.

Was this how all police families operated? I already had the answer to that. I was born into one. Although we had our ups and downs, my father never acted this way. This was definitely something different. But, I still struggled to understand it.

A few years later, my first husband and I divorced. The relationship became toxic. No matter how hard you try, some things cannot be fixed. The emptiness in my gut, the fear of coming home to a successful suicide, walking on eggshells. The sleepless nights, the fear, the humiliation, the threats. I became so scared, I feared for my life when driving in the car with him and would physically feel nauseous and tremble. I felt betrayed and devastated. I needed to get out of the marriage for my sake and for my children.

In 2009, I graduated from college with honors, a scholarship and an award, and found part-time employment as a paramedic with two services. I felt confident that I knew all about what PTSD was and how the traumatic and stressful events a first responder experiences affects their well-being. While in college, I had researched and composed an essay on this very issue, PTSD and first responder family. Sadly, the reality of the powerful stigma and the 'old boys' club mentality was stronger than I could have imagined. But, where I was with my marriage, the pressures and exposures I was facing on the job was a whole new ball game.

Even so, I thought I had everything under control. I had already had PTSD and won, I could handle this...

Due to some unsettling personal events in my earlier years, I was diagnosed with PTSD a full nine years before I began my career as a first responder. I had no idea my quick temper, almost uncontrollable rage, and depressive episodes were abnormal. This was all I knew. This was my life. There were many times when I would have suicidal ideations. It's a terrifying place to be, I felt numb most of the time, and I cried daily. I lacked the precious privilege of simple 'joy' in my life. I missed my best friend terribly who died as a result of a car accident when I was seventeen. I went to the cemetery weekly, sometimes more often, and I spent hours there. Talking to her, mourning her, mourning the void in my life. Something was missing. There was a huge void, a nothingness in my life that I could just not fix. And so, I carried on. What else was I to do? This was life as I knew it. I was damaged goods. This was as good as it was going to get for me, and I accepted this.

As I began my career as a first responder, I was excited at the opportunity to share some of the information and resources that I had acquired in college, through the charity that had awarded me with a scholarship. I knew intimately what it was like to live with PTSD and wanted to help others learn about what it was, the warning signs, and to know they were not alone.

Sadly, neither service was interested in mental health education. At one of the services I was told by the deputy chief, "We have our own way of dealing with that." A number of years later, that same service had seen one paramedic attempt suicide, and another who was successful. At the funeral, I so badly wanted to scream at the deputy chief, "You've got this, do you?" I made the wise decision to keep that thought to myself. I had put up some posters and brochures about mental health initiatives on the bulletin boards at the paramedic bases in an effort to offer an anonymous solution for someone hurting. They were all quickly taken down. Frustrated and, as a new employee, lacking confidence as well as feeling the powerful hold of the stigma, I stopped talking about mental health at work. I continued to advocate for the charity, which provided me with so many opportunities. I traveled across Canada in support of the charity, explaining how it works. I felt privileged to speak about mental health, sharing with first responders the programs, research projects and support services offered.

Sadly, I had become too disillusioned to talk about mental health initiatives for first responders at home. I struggled with this for a number of years because I could see people hurting, but held back by the stigma. The number of public safety personnel suicides seemed to be growing exponentially. I often say to colleagues, it's not a matter of *IF* something is going to happen, but *WHEN*.

In 2014, I was invited to be a part of a cross Canada tour with the charity, educating on first responder mental health. One of the stops on the tour was the city where I served. This terrified me. It's one thing to speak to a room full of not-so-strange-strangers; it's entirely different to speak to a room full of colleagues about mental health. I was part of the planning committee and was assigned a chair on stage as part of a discussion panel. The event had a successful turnout of around three-hundred people. It was the first workshop provided in my city for first responder mental health, and I was thrilled to be a part of it. That summer evening presentation is where first responder support started, and where it ended. I had so hoped that someone in the community would take it upon themselves to provide further education, as there was a clear need and positive response to this focus. That did not happen.

As a first responder, I suffered for a number of years in silence. I wasn't listening to my soul. I wasn't allowing myself to get the help and support that I needed to be well. This, in turn, wasn't fair to the people closest to me. I was too busy to listen to my inner voice, and I was too convinced by the stigma to take action. That all changed a few years ago.

When I first started out as a paramedic, it was difficult to obtain full-time employment. In the first years, I worked as many as four jobs at a time, (two with paramedic services, one with an events medical service, and one working as a first aid instructor), just to make ends meet. Shortly after I gained employment with my first paramedic service, I became a single parent. I had to figure out quickly how I was going to support myself plus my two kids as a single mom.

I was running myself ragged. My health began to deteriorate and, as a result of the stress that I had been experiencing, life became difficult. Medical issues started to present themselves first. I lacked sleep, self-care, and downtime. I was responsible for my two young children, their activities, getting them to and from school. At the time, sleep wasn't the most important thing. Paying bills and putting food on the table was. I had no backup. I was fully responsible for all aspects of our lives, and I was numb.

As a result, there were countless injuries on the job due to exhaustion, overuse, strains, and sprains. I continued to work on modified duties while in recovery, but that was a catch-22. You feel like you should be 'on the road', and as a result, often return to full duties prematurely. The stigma and disapproval from your fellow colleagues while on modified is almost unbearable.

During my early years as a paramedic, I faced a skin and cervical cancer diagnosis as well as debilitating migraine and benign migraine symptoms. I worked through most of that without any time off or downtime to recover. I was part-time; if I didn't work, I didn't get paid. I had far greater responsibilities to take care of besides my health. Or so I thought. Some of the injuries I sustained earlier in my career continue to haunt me every once-in-awhile. When I'm off on modified duty, yet again, I sometimes kid with my co-workers and say, "It's time to put my modified tiara back on." This is a deflection. A sarcastic coping mechanism I use to cover up the embarrassment and humiliation I experience while on modified duty.

I made the choice of not listening to the warning signs my body was screaming at me, because I didn't know what they were, and because I was just too busy. Generally speaking, a mental health injury doesn't just show up one day. Instead, it starts slowly and insidiously creeps into your life. Before you know it, it has taken over everything. It is difficult to even recognize this happening because you are so caught up in just trying to keep afloat. At the beginning of my career, it took some serious illnesses to shake me up and get me to notice that I was indeed in trouble.

Once I gained full-time employment, I left the other paramedic service. With just one full-time job, my hope was to add some balance to my life. It was a good choice, but at the same time, it was terrifying. I had to come to terms with the fact that I would be making considerably less money and adjusted accordingly. I had to learn to stop feeling guilty for not always 'doing something', for not always being at work. It took over a year for me to settle into my new life, working one job and one service. Once I finally settled in, I couldn't figure out why it took me so long to take this positive step!

I continued my mental health advocacy work, volunteering where I could, participating in education, conferences, and seminars, and I started to grow. I had finally slowed down enough to allow myself space and time to pursue counseling, to practice self-care. Not only that, I began horseback riding again, had time to ski, or simply go for walks with my dogs. I was hitting the gym three to five times a week. As a result of this, injuries at work decreased. I was feeling stronger both mentally and physically. I felt very grateful that I was able to do for myself. I slowly started to recognize some of the signs and symptoms that I previously had been exhibiting and started to take preventative action earlier. I was able to hear my family's concerns, not just listen to what they were telling me. I began to understand they were only trying to tell me out of love. But, now I understood why.

One cold January day, a couple of years after I resigned from my second paramedic service, I received a text message from one of my former colleagues. He reached out to tell me that one of our fellow paramedics had died by suicide. The news could not have been more devastating. I felt cold. I felt numb again. I struggled with this loss tremendously even though I was no longer working there.

This paramedic and I had never been exceptionally close, but we would say hello to each other, passing by in hallways or while waiting at the hospitals. This individual was well liked and, from the outside, seemed well balanced. It was a tremendous shock to me. I couldn't even fathom what this loss meant to his family, colleagues, and friends.

Although I had been practicing self -care, the job of a paramedic has a way of throwing potholes into the road as you make your way through the constant exposure to trauma and suffering through the course of the job. At the time of the news, I wasn't exceptionally healthy.

The Mental Health Commission of Canada offers a course called Road to Mental Readiness. As a way of identifying how much stress you are under, they developed the Mental Health Continuum. Stress levels are represented by the colors green, yellow, orange, and red. At the green end of the spectrum, you are considered healthy. Yellow represents reasonably healthy coping. Orange is a warning area where the individual is starting to exhibit behaviors, signs, and symptoms of not coping well. Things like self-medicating with alcohol or drugs, angry outbursts, uncontrollable crying can be seen here. The red section represents those who are suffering from an injury and are well into a crisis point. People in this category are often diagnosed by a medical practitioner as having a mental health illness. Examples of this are anxiety, depression and post-traumatic stress injury (PTSI), to list a few. I was probably in the orange category at the time of the suicide. Afterward, I was definitely in the red zone.

I suffered from something called misplaced guilt. My faulty thought process was that I had known of these conditions, yet I believed that I had failed to share this information with my colleagues. I experienced some very dark times in the weeks after. Once the grief and anger stage had passed, I felt I had to do something.

Provoked by this tragedy, I decided that I could no longer keep this potentially lifesaving information to myself. I needed to be brave enough to speak publicly about mental health injuries and illnesses. I was no longer willing to hide behind the stigma. I spoke to a few friends that I had made through my advocacy work and told them I was going to start speaking. I began working on the story of my personal journey again, sharing the road that led to my resilience, in order to help people like me who were afraid to reach out. I suspect that most first responders came into this career as a result of experiencing some type of adverse experience in their lives. Exposure to traumatic events can create a strong drive in an individual to take action, a desire to make an impact. There is a strong need to make changes in order to prevent people from suffering the same struggles.

I took a leap of faith and agreed to speak at an event in Nova Scotia called Helping the Helpers. I was no longer Stef the medic, or Stef the PTSD survivor. I became Stef the advocate! On stage, I felt confident. I was simply telling my story. I just had to state the facts. I was overwhelmed with a sense of accomplishment, I felt as if a light bulb had been switched on. I was no longer silent or hiding who I was. I became empowered by this experience of speaking out and tremendously humbled to have been able to share my message. My confidence has grown with each engagement opportunity I am invited to present. The power of speech is addictive and fierce. It matches my passion for raising awareness about first responder mental health. I have a new outlook on my path moving forward. I now see myself as brave, a trendsetter, a pioneer, a fierce warrior.

After I have finished speaking, I am often approached by a number of individuals who thank me for speaking out. I have become someone they look up to, someone they can learn from, someone who is willing to be vulnerable and real with them. Someone who is only getting louder!

There is nothing quite like the feeling you get when you receive a standing ovation. My heart is overjoyed with gratitude and purpose. It gives me a sense of accomplishment and hope for first responders, the culture and our future. People want to hear our adversity stories, they want to learn from them. To make it a better place for themselves and others. I am so excited to be making an impact and promoting change within our culture.

A few months later, I became a contributor to a book compilation that went international bestseller in one day! All I had to do was share a bit of my story with the readers. This again helped to quash any doubts I had about myself.

Speaking has ignited a passion in me that I didn't know I had. It felt great to be stomping out stigma across Canada, but my issue remained. More still needed to be done *at home*.

In May 2017, I became the founder of a Wings of Change peer support group for first responders and frontline workers. During these meetings, we participate in anonymous, solution-based discussion and education regarding any work-related trauma and mental health challenges. We always refrain from any triggering 'trauma-talk'. ALL types of first responders are welcome; be they career, retired, or volunteer. The Brantford Wings of Change chapter has now been running strong for sixteen months!

In February 2018, I presented to a large international group of first responders at a prestigious education week and symposium on PTSD and mental health in Toronto, Ontario. With this momentum behind me, I knew I had to bring this type of education and workshop experience home to my colleagues and allied agencies.

Stigma creates so many barriers for first responders facing PTSD or OSI's. One of the many barriers in my area is the lack of support. We *are* different, and we need a more customized program to address our needs. So, I created the Stefanie Speaks COMMUNITY. I had no idea what it was going to become, but I had the drive to start. I stepped out in faith, scared to death of what my colleagues were going to think, scared to fail. But the need was far bigger than my fear.

On June 19, 2018, I presented an exclusive screening of the film-documentary *The Other Side of the Hero*. This film was created to bring awareness to the public and first responder world about mental health injuries. The event sold out! I was overwhelmed and proud, and this confirmed the need for this type of support in my community.

In September 2018, I launched a new program combining equine-assisted learning and informal peer support. I have received offers to speak internationally for 2019. It's amazing the doors that open when you're on the right path.

In November 2018, Stefanie Speaks is providing a workshop titled Helping the Helpers - Focus on the Family. Recalling what it was like being the spouse and daughter of a police officer, not knowing how to get help, feeling like no one understood, I am proud to now be part of the solution.

Resistance to resilience is not an easy journey. It took me a lot of hard work and many tears. Growth through adversity is focused and deliberate. The pain of adversity can be transformed into a beautiful strength if supported and treated with care. My lived experience has created a fierce drive in me to help others.

I am grateful for my past. I look forward to my future. I feel privileged to have taken all the resistance in my own life and turned it into a resiliency that allows me to reach out to others and create positive change.

Awilda Prignano

Awilda is a transformational coach that helps individuals become the best version of themselves through lasting habit change and self-care. She is currently working on obtaining her Neuro-Linguistic Programming practitioner certification to further her study and understanding of the human experience, communication, and behavior.

Awilda has co-authored books with Follow It Thru Publishing – *Obstacles Equal Opportunities* and *The Real Journey of the Empowered MomBoss*.

In 2019, Awilda is fulfilling a life-long dream and will be traveling internationally with a group of professionals via Remote Year. She is looking forward to immersing herself in the various cultural experiences and growing both personally and professionally by collaborating with like-minded individuals.

Find Awilda online:

awildawrites@gmail.com
https://www.instagram.com/laboricuagurl
https://twitter.com/LaBoricuaGurl

Releasing the Monkey

By Awilda Prignano

A girl's first influence and most important role model is her mother. Growing up, I always saw my mother as a beautiful woman and the perfect homemaker. She was an amazing cook, and our house was always immaculately clean. She was not just a pretty face, but also the authoritarian in our family. She had very strict rules when it came to our house. We were allowed in the living and dining rooms only when company was over. The upholstered furniture was covered in plastic. Allowing us to have friends over was a rare treat. My mother cherished and took very good care of our home and everything in it. In her words, she and my father worked very hard for us to have nice things. Our way of showing appreciation and gratitude was to acknowledge this and be respectful of their (her) wishes. I sometimes jokingly describe the house I grew up in as a cross between a church and furniture store—everything EXACTLY in its place. This may all seem unusual, but this was our world—*her* things, *her* house, *her* rules. We never challenged her word and would follow the rules to a tee. My mother was also extremely perceptive—nothing ever got past her. She was the parent that did most, if not all, of the disciplining. Dare to cross her, and we'd feel the burn of whatever was within her reach. In our home, Mom was the enforcer of tough love.

Parents are the first to shape our world, so naturally, their ideas and values are embedded deep inside our hearts and our minds. Words and how they're spoken hold so much power. For many years, my mother's voice was the one I heard in my head telling me what was right and what was wrong. She'd been my biggest fan as well as my absolute worst and harshest critic. At times, it could be too much 'tough love' to swallow. It would be many years before I would realize how the impact of those words, embedded deep within me, would have an effect on my confidence and mindset, even as an adult.

Within a few years, circumstances changed dramatically within my family. My father became very ill, and my mother was his primary caregiver. My husband had suddenly passed away, and I was left to raise my then thirteen-month-old daughter as a single working mom. At a time when a mother and daughter should be coming closer together, I felt like our relationship was falling apart. I was trying to do my best, and I knew I had to work to support myself and my daughter. My mother had her own hands full with caring for my father and dealing with everything as best she could. This was a time when our family was in dire need of love, support and understanding for each other. Unfortunately, this would be easier said than done.

As times became more challenging in my parent's household, I saw my mother become more difficult and intolerable to deal with. She had an extremely short temper, and it didn't take much to set it off. I could see how her moodiness was a direct reflection of the challenges she was facing in her own home. I couldn't help but feel that, at times, I was an easy target for her and too emotionally weak to defend myself against her. Her criticism and negativity towards me just seemed to hurt in ways that made me feel broken. She would comment on my appearance, make rude remarks about my weight gain due to stress and criticized my lack of homemaking skills. I was nowhere near the cook or perfect homemaker she was. It was during this time I felt the need to distance myself from my mother so that we could each have the space we needed to adjust to our circumstances. The farther I was from her and her negative energy, the better I could function and deal with my own situation.

This, of course, led to what I could best describe as a complicated relationship between my mother and me. This went on for years. It wasn't like we never saw each other, though. My mom really enjoyed being a grandmother. Two days a week, she would help care for my daughter while I was at work. I'm grateful for the time they spent together, as my mother was a great influence on her. She taught my daughter to speak Spanish and accustomed her to the food and culture of our Puerto Rican heritage. Seeing the happiness in my daughter's face and knowing my parents would look forward to her visits made the whole situation tolerable for me. And sometimes in those moments, I would feel a bit deprived of the patience and love she showed my daughter as the dynamic between me and my mother had always been different.

As the years went by, my father's condition progressed, and my mom held on, doing the best she could as his caregiver. My parents had downsized to a condo and moved into the one on the floor just above me. I was happy to have my parents close by so I could be available to them as they needed me. I also appreciated their continued support with childcare for my daughter. My relationship with my mother wasn't much different, but I learned to keep my guard up and maintain my distance as needed. As confident as I felt on a daily basis holding down my own as a single working mom, my mother could sometimes throw zingers my way that would just break my heart and deflate my spirit.

Living as neighbors, I was close enough to see how difficult and stressful being a caregiver became for my mom on a daily basis.

To break her from her regular routine, I started taking her to the movies, dinners, shopping and even getting our nails done together. In those moments, having my mother to myself, I started to see the lovely and funny person that she was when she wasn't under so much stress. These became moments that we both enjoyed and would look forward to.

Shortly after my parents had moved into the condo, my father had a desire to travel. He knew his condition wasn't improving, and he wanted to take a trip with my mother while they still had the means and he was physically able to travel. He shared with me his idea, and I took him to a travel agent to review trips and discuss options. He was fixated on a sixteen-day cruise that started in Tampa and traveled to Columbia, the Panama Canal, four stops in Mexico, Los Angeles and finished in Vancouver, Canada. He'd never been to any of those places and was excited at the thought of traveling and exploring new territories. He couldn't wait to go home and share the news with my mom.

My mother was dead against it, as she didn't see the need to spend so much money. I tried to intervene and get her to see it through his eyes. She wouldn't budge. A few days later, he came down to my place and said, "I'll pay for you if you pay for your kid. I really want to go. I *need* to go. Let's do it!" I saw the excitement in his eyes. His face was lit up. His smile was ear to ear. I couldn't say no. I was excited for him as I was for my daughter and me to travel. I hated to come between my parents like that, but I knew in my heart it was the right thing to do. It was what he wanted and needed at the time to feel like he was participating in something else other than the mundane moments of day to day life.

Even after all these years, I do not regret taking that trip with my dad. My whole life, I'd only seen my dad as a strong, hard-working and very dedicated husband and father. He gave so much of himself so we could have everything we needed and wanted. This time, he was asking for something he wanted, and it was upsetting to me that my mother couldn't see it—or at least feel it in her heart like I did. My father's health had slowly been deteriorating, but on that ship, I saw him move, dance and enjoy himself in a way I hadn't seen in a long time. I don't know if it was the ambiance, the sunshine, the sea air or just the freedom he felt in his heart, but during the time on that cruise ship, I saw him so happy and full of energy.

In those sixteen days, there wasn't one day that went by that he didn't mention my mother, how much he loved her, and how he wished she was there to enjoy this experience with him. Seeing my father yearn for my mother in this way, I could feel how deep his love was for her. My own feelings for her were already complex. Witnessing the anguish she caused him with her decision just made me see her as selfish at a time when she could have been more loving and understanding of his needs. After so many years, that sentiment still breaks my heart.

A few years later, one early September morning, my mother called me in a panic, telling me I needed to rush upstairs. She couldn't wake my father up. We called the paramedics, and he was immediately transported to the hospital.

As he slept overnight, he had fallen into a coma and never came back to us again. My father was the strongest man I'd ever known and had a very strong will to live. He held on for eight days in the hospital before his organs finally gave out. My mother and I were there with him as he took his last breath. His suffering was finally over. On Sept. 11, 2001, our nation suffered a great tragedy. Our family suffered a personal loss of our own as my dad passed away in the early morning hours on that day. It's difficult to describe being there in that moment losing someone you love so much. My dad was, and will forever be, my hero.

In the next few months after my father's passing, my daughter and I moved from the condo. I needed change and new surroundings. I found an adorable townhome in an area about half hour away. Just close enough to be there if my mom needed anything and far enough to feel the peace and tranquility I was craving.

For the first time in her life, my mother had no one to take care of but herself. She found the local senior center where they offered activities, classes and events she could attend. It was there that she found friendships and a new purpose for her life. She now had a social calendar that filled her days. My mother also had two brothers she was very close to and enjoyed spending time with. As time progressed, she eventually lost each of them to cancer and was never the same again. Her heart was completely broken. The men in her life that she depended on for strength were gone.

I had been laid off from work and decided to take a trip a short time thereafter. When I returned, I came over to spend some time with my mother. Right away, I noticed a difference in her behavior. She was constantly repeating herself. The house wasn't kept as it usually had been and seemed a bit disheveled. This was rare for my mom, as all her life she prided herself in keeping an immaculate home. Over the next few months, when I visited her, I noticed her condition was becoming worse. She started collecting and accumulating items around her house that just didn't make sense—newspapers, magazines and various other items that were just trash. My mother remained active at the senior center and went almost daily. Even though she lived alone, my mother had friends that checked in on her regularly and were as close as a phone call away should she need anything.

A little over a year later, my situation had changed, and I ended up putting my belongings into storage and moving in with my mother. She had been asking me to do so for a while, as she was having difficulty dealing with housekeeping tasks and managing her finances. She also shared she was scared of being alone. As much as I disliked the idea of moving in with her, it was what we both needed as I wasn't working at the time.

In a strange sense, it seemed the challenges I had experienced that year were meant to happen so that I could be with my mom when she needed me most. After a period of various tests, my mother was diagnosed with moderate Lewy body dementia. My thoughts immediately went to, *What is that? What does this all mean?*

Regardless of how many books there are explaining exactly what is happening, nothing can really protect you from the emotional rollercoaster and mental drain of what it's like to experience this awful disease first-hand. At a time when I was expected to be resilient, I was instead feeling confused, angry and scared. The doctor advised me not to wait too long to take the next steps, as this condition could progress rapidly. He also shared something that made it easier for me to deal with my mom's prognosis. Patients with dementia start to see everything around them as very distorted. They are easily confused, forgetful and lose the ability to reason. He explained to me when a situation with my mom would come up where I would get angry or frustrated, try to reason and resolve it with her as I would a five-year-old. This for me was huge. This picture he just painted not only clarified what I needed to know to move forward, but also how vulnerable a position my mother was in.

The first task was being named my mother's power of attorney. I had spoken to my mother about this and explained to her what this role was. I made sure to select a bilingual individual to handle the proceeding to ensure my mother was in full understanding and an active part of the process. Next, with the help of Catholic Charities, I was able to place my mother in adult daycare for a few hours during the week while I was at work. This was a major adjustment, but once all the kinks were worked out, it became a place she enjoyed spending time with new acquaintances.

Knowing the dementia was progressing, I wanted to make sure to create moments and have conversations with my mother before it would all change. There was one evening we went out to dinner to one of her favorite restaurants. When our plates were brought out, a look came over her face of disgust. I asked what was wrong, and she said she didn't like what was brought to her and refused to eat it. I told her she did like it, and we ordered exactly what she wanted. I remembered what the doctor said about how to handle the situation. I asked her what about the dish she didn't like. She said, "All this stuff" as she pointed at the mushrooms in the sauce. I then asked, "If I take them off, will you eat it?" She agreed. She finished the whole plate.

Not every situation was so easy to resolve and some, more painful to process. She would come at me at times and accuse me of stealing her money, taking her things, and she started hiding food around the house. I would wake up at 3 am to the sound of her banging pots and completely reorganizing everything in the kitchen cabinets. When there is no control, there is also no filter. She couldn't control what was coming out of her mouth. I felt myself reliving some of those hurtful blows from our past. My patience was wearing thin. My life was minimized to working and then coming home to this situation. I would tell myself, *Just breathe. I'm just a daughter trying to do the best I can for my mom.* It was all I could do to try and get through it day to day.

Adult day care was only during the week, so my mom was at home on the weekends. One Saturday evening, I came home from work to a dark house. It was unusual, but I figured maybe my mom was out with a friend or family member as had been the case in the past. As I was cooking dinner, I received a call from the emergency room. The nurse on the phone explained my mom was there and wanted me to go pick her up. When I got there, my mother was being treated for cuts and bruises. She had been found fallen on a sidewalk, and paramedics brought her in. They had run x-rays and checked her over to ensure everything else was okay. On the car ride home, I asked her why she left the house. She wouldn't give me an answer. The next day, she did the same thing, only this time her injuries were more serious. Her jaw was broken in two places. Her chin was purple from cuts and bruises, and she needed stitches. My mother could no longer be left home alone. She needed full-time care.

With assistance from the caseworker at the hospital, she was placed in an assisted living facility. For a while, I'd been trying to find accommodation for her that would be a better fit, but just couldn't afford it. It took an incident like this to happen to finally get the assistance needed to place her where she would get the full-time care she needed. I don't think I'll ever get over the guilt of having my mom in assisted living. This is the absolute worst form of tough love for anyone to live through.

The time came to start clearing my mom's place. This was a task I was dreading to do as even though many years before my parents had downsized from house to condo, my mom still had a lot of stuff. I tackled this project room by room. The room I left for last was her bedroom. My mom spent a lot of her time in her bedroom, and I could still feel her energy among some of her things.

Looking around and going through, two things stood out. One, my mom collected a lot of religious artifacts. There were crosses, statues and prayer cards all over the place. She also had an old bible and quite a collection of prayer books. It's strange to say this, but I don't think having these things ever brought my mother any peace or comfort. Second, when going through family pictures, I noticed in pictures with my father, we would be hugging, kissing and laughing with him...clearly happy times.

In most pictures with my mom, she was barely smiling. In fact, she seemed sad and miserable. It was a realization I wasn't expecting. Looking at these pictures, I no longer saw my mother as my mom, but as a woman suffering from some kind of sadness I didn't know of or understand. At that moment, looking through all those pictures, all I could feel was compassion for her. This woman that had caused me so much pain with her words was a person who was going through her own pain. Expressing herself in the way that she did was probably the only way she knew how to release it. In my mind, this didn't make it okay; it just made it make sense.

I go with her to all her doctor's appointments, and at every visit, her doctor will ask her questions to access her cognitive skills. When he points at me, he'll ask, "Who is this?" My mom will say, "That's my daughter," or call me by name. At our last visit, the doctor asked her, "Who is this?" and pointed at me. And then it happened...that moment came.

"I don't know..." she said.

Hearing her say those words broke me. I started to well up. It was all I could do without completely breaking down.

Nowadays, I see her at the assisted care facility as she sits so frail among her friends. Looking back at our life, the complexity of our relationship can't be denied. With time and perspective, I can rationalize my mother was only trying to do her best. Her lashing out was her way of releasing pain and stress. With time, I've learned to let go and choose to move forward. I do this for me. In the end, all we have left is love.

Being my mother's caregiver has been the most frustrating, exhausting and tormenting experience I have had the honor and privilege to do. I may have lost her to dementia, but she is still here, with me in the present. She may no longer know who I am, but I know exactly who she is... my dear mother.

Awilda González Reyes

Awilda González Reyes is a Puerto Rican writer, with a background in mental health and workforce development. She has dedicated her career assisting clients to become self-reliant by defining, pursuing and achieving their own goals.

As a mother and a grandmother, Awilda is familiar with the struggles in parenting, having a career and maintaining her own identity. She is an author in the #1 international bestseller, *The Real Journey of the Empowered Momboss*, has been published in Gozamos.com and was a featured poet at Proyecto Latina. In 2013, two poems closest to her heart, *Allegiance* and *Endangered Species*, were published in Rebeldes: A Proyecto Latina Anthology. Awilda was also a content writer for *The Body Is Not an Apology* from November 2014 – August 2015.

She is currently turning life challenges into triumphs through motivational speaking, delving into her blog Atentamente Awilda, and building a legacy that moves, touches, and inspires others into their best life.

Find Awilda online:

www.instagram.com/awildagr/
www.atentamenteawilda.wordpress.com
https://www.linkedin.com/in/awildagonzalez/

What's Hair Got to do With It?

By Awilda González Reyes

They say the only thing constant is change, and yet, we resist the changes with every fiber of our being. We resist all types from the moment we're born, we come out crying, not just boohoo tears, but hysterically crying. If a baby could really talk I'm almost sure they would be screaming things like, "Put me back in"; "Why is there so much light"; "I want to be back in the comfort of my mommy's womb." I'm sure newborn babies want what we all want: safety, comfort, and security.

We find security in everything remaining just the way we like it, but if change is constant in our lives, does everything really remain the same? Perhaps some things can remain the same, the things we have control over might remain. However, how much of our life do we really control, or is our attempt to resist change merely a false sense of security? I know, I'm getting deep and philosophical; for me, it's in these moments of diving deeper that I find freedom even in the process of resisting the change that I really have no control over.

My life has been a whirlwind of change. I can honestly say it's been a constant in my life. Have there been moments where I challenged and resisted the change? Of course, it's part of human nature. I have found that the harder I resist, or the longer I prolong facing the change, that's where I find conflict within my spirit. I end up harming myself rather than helping. I could probably write a whole book on the many changes and moments of adversity that I have faced, but this time I want to focus on just one area of my life, hair...

From a very young age, we are conditioned to think a certain way, be a certain way, live a certain way. We are taught what is deemed normal, beautiful or accepted. I am from the Caribbean, specifically from the island of Puerto Rico. Growing up, I had super long hair. The type that flows in the wind on a summer breezy day, you know, like in the commercials we see that promote hair products. Long, past my waist—luscious thick, black hair.

As a very young girl, maybe as early as four, I remember how my grandmother would await my arrival to Puerto Rico on our yearly family visit. What made these trips so special was that I always knew Mama Julia would greet me with a special gift. Every year without fail she would make sure that I had new, fresh ponytail holders. These were not just any ponytail holders, they were special; well, at least they were special to me. They looked like huge colorful marbles that shined like a rainbow, and they were all mine, chosen especially for me.

In the afternoons, I would visit my grandmother, and she would brush my long hair with her own hairbrush. I remember how important it was for her, to create the perfect ponytail for me, every single hair in place, total perfection. I believe that was the first time I learned of the importance of my long black straight hair.

Later on, around the age of eight or nine, the texture of my hair began to change. It was no longer straight, but wavy. That beach wave look that many women now pay to create were the waves my mother wanted to tame. That's when she began to iron my hair. Yes, you read that correctly—iron. Back in the day, there were no flat irons, so we had to use the next best thing, an iron, or my personal favorite, hair rollers bigger than a can of corn. This became a weekly ritual with my mother. It was important to keep that long straight hair because anything other than that meant I had "bad hair," or so I was led to believe. I hated those rollers with a passion, and I hated that iron just as much. Having such long thick hair meant I would have to keep the rollers on all day, and sometimes until the next day. Needless to say, sleeping was painful and incredibly uncomfortable. Yet, this is what I had to endure to keep the "bad hair" tamed and to be seen as beautiful.

My adolescent years came with hormonal changes, and you guessed it, my hair changed once again around the age of twelve. It was at this time that I was finally allowed to cut my hair for the first time ever. In an act of rebelliousness, I decided to cut it really short rather than just trimming it! That's when the texture of my hair changed even more. I went from having tamed straight hair to tight coiled "pelo malo" (bad) curly hair. I still remember some of my grammar school pictures during those years. At the time, I hated them.

My mom's approach to my hair care changed, and our mother/daughter rituals went from ironing and rollers to chemical straightening treatments. It was like clockwork every three months, our customary trip to the local salon to chemically strip me of my "bad hair." It was either too curly, or it was so chemically straightened, that it felt like wire. There were times my hair had become so brittle that the chemicals would burn chunks away, making my "bad hair" look even worse.

This process continued for years until I moved from home and took control. At first, it took a long time for me to learn to even deal with my hair. All I knew is that I was done with the years of chemical straightening. I knew I wanted to embrace my waves and curls that were controlled for so long. However, I struggled with the years of not knowing which image of myself I wanted to embrace. Did I want to embrace the curly haired woman or the straight-haired woman?

I had moments where I went straight all the time by pulling my hair with round huge brushes and flattening with a flat iron, a quick and easy fix. I also went through moments where I left my hair curly, but those were the days that I was reminded that my hair looked better straight, so I was back to square one. It felt like a constant identity crisis, and I was growing tired of it.

Everything changed when finally, I began to learn who I was culturally. Reading about my cultural history and identity began to open my eyes to a world that had not existed growing up. The more I learned, the more curious I became about my ancestors. I began to ask questions about my ancestral lineage, who were my great grandparents, where did they come from, and what did they look like?

There it was, as clear as day; reality was that I didn't have to choose one over the other. That having curly hair really didn't mean that I had "pelo malo," and having straight hair did not mean my curls were less worthy. I could embrace both because both were who I was. My great grandparents were the real key to my freedom and the end of my love-hate relationship with my hair. They all had different hair textures because they all came from different ethnic backgrounds. African, Taino, and Spaniard! Finally, this explained how I could easily change from straight hair to wavy and wild curls.

For so long, I hated my hair and resisted accepting my reality, but when I learned to love my ancestral diversity, I learned to love what my hair represented. It no longer symbolized pain for me, it symbolized a rich background that I was so eagerly seeking for a long time. It symbolized my own acceptance of myself and my ancestors. I felt so honored to have such a gift from them.

Unfortunately, unlearning messages we learn during our youth can take years and years of peeling back the layers, of negative talk and thoughts that have been embedded in our mind and souls.

You may think that this is where my journey with my hair ended. Little did I know that years later, as an adult, my view on hair and beauty would go through another change. Remember what I said in the beginning, the only thing constant is change? Well, I was about to face the biggest change.

In 2014, at the ripe age of forty-six, I had long curly beautiful thick locks. I loved my hair so much. I can honestly say that at that time, I was a bit vain, always buying products to maintain the beautiful coils and making sure that none were out of place. It was also during the time that a lot happened in my life, and I experienced high levels of stress. Between parenting challenges, navigating a career and being a caretaker for an ill fiancée, I didn't know if I was coming or going half of the time. Yet, I always looked put together and portrayed the image that I was living a life that was rosy. I was internalizing so much emotional pain that I went through the deepest depression I have ever felt.

In April of 2014, during a trip, I was getting ready for an event, and that's when I noticed a quarter sized bald spot on the right side of my head. I had never noticed it before because I usually left my hair curly, but this time I had decided to blow dry my hair straight. I was scared and confused, so as soon as I returned home,

I went to see my physician. I had spent years with many other symptoms, but all it took was one blood test to determine I had Hashimoto's disease. My first reaction was, "I have hashi what!?"

Hashimoto's disease is an autoimmune disorder in which your immune system creates antibodies that damage your thyroid gland. In other words, your own immune system attacks itself, and typically progresses slowly over the years, causing chronic thyroid damage, along with hair loss. As the months progressed, my hair continued to fall out. There were times I would wake up and see that my pillow was filled with long strands of hair. I would sweep and find hair all over my house. The hardest moments were taking a shower and my hands being filled with clumps of my long hair. I was devastated.

When you have been taught that a woman's hair is her crowning glory, losing it can put you into a state of panic, depression, and fear. Fear that you won't see yourself as beautiful, fear that others will not see you as beautiful, and fear that your partner will not find you beautiful. I was in panic internally, because externally I was still dealing with all the chaos that was happening around me. I didn't allow myself the time to deal with my own illness other than taking the prescribed medication. My girlfriends were the only people I really confided in. I was so scared that I didn't even let my fiancée Johnny know how I felt. How could I? He was dealing with his own sickness, as he had problems with his kidneys.

By the end of 2014, I had lost so much hair that I could see my scalp.

In February 2015, I decided that I was no longer going to be a hostage to what was happening to me. I knew that to move forward, I had to take my power back, which meant cutting off what was left of my hair and not resisting the change. So, I gathered a few girlfriends, and in the privacy of my own bathroom, we cut it all off. I will never forget the fear I felt when I allowed my fiancée to see me bald for the first time. A trillion thoughts went through my mind, and a trillion more feelings engulfed my heart. Would he still think I was beautiful; would society look at me funny? After days of silence followed by a day of discussion, Johnny looked at me and said, "If you think that your hair is what makes you beautiful, then you don't even know your own beauty. It's not your hair that I am in love with."

On February 14, 2015, on Johnny's suggestion, I shaved the buzz cut. I had lost so much hair that my scalp was patchy. I looked like a spotted cheetah.

Fear was still a huge part of my life, I was afraid of going out without covering my bald head. It was then that my BFF set a challenge for me. Thank goodness for amazing women who walk with you in the hardest moments. For thirty days I took a picture and posted it on social media. With each step I took, there was resistance. There were days I looked at myself and just didn't want to deal with my ever-changing appearance, but I pushed past that resistance.

A year later, on February 14, 2016, a lot of my hair had grown back due to steroid injections on my scalp and a change of climate. It was also the day that Johnny passed after a long battle against chronic kidney failure. I was left devastated, lost and confused, like all my dreams had been shattered.

I look back now, and I can clearly see the importance of that day in 2015. Since then, I have lost my hair every year. I am at the point where I have decided to shave off whatever is growing. Resisting and fighting the new me was not going to lead to my freedom, nor was it going to allow me to see the new beauty and strength that passes all understanding—even my own.

Society has placed such an emphasis on women's hair that for those of us that are embracing who we are, it becomes difficult to navigate the stares and assumptions that come with seeing a bald woman. The looks of pity are always the ones that baffle me. Then I realize that they must think I have cancer. I ask myself, would a bald man be under the same scrutiny as a bald woman? There is always a double standard. I know we can get into a debate about it not being common for a woman to be bald, but it still doesn't change how we are perceived.

My journey has been long. However, I am no longer resisting my hair loss; I am now resilient! Just recently, I was given the official diagnosis of alopecia ophiasis, a type of hair loss that is resistant to treatment and is localized to the sides and back of the scalp. My doctor wants to try topical treatment; however, I made it clear that I am fine being who I am—a completely bald bold, beautiful Puerto Rican woman. I have worked through all the feelings, and I have moved past wanting my hair back. I know that I can have hair whenever I want by wearing a wig; there's a selection in my closet right now.

I have consciously decided not to wear a wig, not because I see anything wrong with it, but because it makes me happy. For me, it's more about being an example and a voice for the many women who are suffering in silence, and perhaps using their wigs as a shield. I want to challenge societies' view on beauty. I can be just as beautiful, sexy and professional without hair. Hair is not what makes me presentable or professional. It's not what exudes my confidence or my sexiness. It's quite the contrary. I have finally found the purest beauty in myself through my journey with alopecia. It's the best freedom of love that I can give to myself and to the world.

If you are going through hair loss, here are some of the things you can do to love yourself throughout the process:

Patience: You must learn to be patient with yourself. Be in the moment, be aware of how you feel and run with it. Don't push yourself into doing something that your body just can't do right now. Remember, its temporary, and tomorrow will be better.

Laughter: Laugh through your struggles, because laughter will heal your soul, and in turn, this will heal your body.

Joy in the simple things: Stop and smell the roses, literally! You must find joy in the simplest of moments because every single good moment is a step forward.

Love: Love is what is most important. Love yourself through the trials. Be good to yourself and your body regardless of what is going on. You only have one.

Do the things you love: Surround yourself with the things and people you love the most. When you are going through trials, they will get you through the day.

Know yourself: If you are going through hair loss, know yourself. Knowing yourself and recognizing that what is happening will help you focus and move towards healing.

Knowledge: Educate yourself, ask questions, read books, and look for someone who is going through the same thing for support. Do what feels right to you.

I hope that my journey is a light in yours. I hope that you find freedom in whatever situation you are facing, and I hope that your resistance turns into a triumphant resiliency that makes this world shine a little brighter.

Never forget that you define your beauty. Break through those lessons that hold you back, and free yourself! The world will be a better place because of it.

As for what's next for me, we shall see. Change is constant, and I'm always open to the next step in my journey.

My biggest desire is to free myself of everything I have been led to believe, so that I can, in turn, free the minds of others. I no longer live in fear, and that, dear reader, is the freedom that comes with resiliency.

Vera Stark

Vera is a spiritual life coach, soul realignment practitioner, and intuitive energy healer. She lives in British Columbia, Canada with her husband. Through a tremendous desire and determination to overcome her own life situations, Vera used her ability to heal herself from the emotional trauma she was experiencing. As a result of her own growth and healing, she realized by changing her inner world, she was experiencing a different outer world. This was a defining moment in her decision to pursue her passion as a spiritual life coach and energy healer.

Vera has worked with hundreds of women on a global scale, helping them to transform their lives, spiritually, emotionally and physically. Her diversified skills have helped her to assist her clients through their difficulties, so they can create a more empowered life for themselves.

Find Vera online:

www.secretsofthesoul.ca
https://www.facebook.com/secretsofthesoul.ca

The Missing Piece Inside of Me

By Vera Stark

Somehow, I always knew that there was more out there that I hadn't yet discovered. I used to think about what it might be, but never realized the truth of it all until much later in my life as my journey unfolded.

I grew up on a farm in Southern Ontario, the eldest of six kids. My parents worked hard, and although they didn't have a lot of money, they did the best they could to make sure we always had food on the table and clothes on our back.

I had a good childhood and a supportive family, yet I always felt as if something in my life was missing. It wasn't something I could explain, nor would I ever have told anyone. I was quite shy back then and sharing my feelings wasn't something that came naturally to me. In fact, it was something I would most often avoid.

My parents were both religious, so going to church on Sundays was a family ritual. We would dress up in our Sunday best, hop in the old brown station wagon, and off we'd go. I never really enjoyed going to church for the simple fact that I didn't like sitting that long and I didn't understand a word that was being said. The sermons went way over my head. It's funny how much you retain even when you don't understand it.

I remember as a child my mom would sit on the side of my bed every night and teach me to pray. I wasn't really sure why at first, but as I grew older, praying became really important to me.

I went to Catholic school right up until high school and even attended summer school for a couple of years, where I was taught by the nuns. I began to understand more about religion, the church, and God. Some of it was very frightening for me.

The older I became, and the more I began to understand and observe, the more questions I had.

I learned a lot of beliefs about God as I was growing up. I always thought He was someone who would punish me if I did something wrong, which had always frightened me. I remember swearing once as a little girl and my mom telling me that if I swore again, God would punish me. He didn't like little girls who swore apparently. My mom had her own beliefs at that time that she also had learned during her childhood. My first thought when my mom said that was, God doesn't love me. I remember feeling very sad and disappointed in myself at the time. Growing up, I always felt that I had to do everything perfectly, and even then, I never believed it was ever good enough. Even at a young age, I was questioning my decisions, wondering if what I was doing was right or wrong. There were times when I felt completely lost and unsure of what I should or shouldn't do.

Even in school, I would never put up my hand to answer a question for fear it would be wrong. I always worried about what everyone else would think, so rather than express my true feelings, I would say what I felt others wanted to hear and wanted me to do. That's what made me feel accepted. I was one of those children who was the last to be picked by the other kids for anything we did in school. I never felt loved. It was a painful experience to go through. I knew my family loved me, but to me, that was different. I just believed that that's what families do.

Religion taught me many things growing up. Anything that was seen by the church as bad was a sin, and God would punish me if I sinned. I learned about Heaven and Hell at a very young age, and how God chose who would go to Heaven and who would go to Hell. I carried this belief for many years and was always terrified of dying or losing anyone close to me.

As a child, I was led to believe that when we die, we either go to Heaven or to Hell. If I was good, I would go to Heaven to be with God, and if I was bad, I would go to Hell and live with the devil. That was a pretty scary thought for a child. As I write and think back on this, I realize how devastating this must have been for me. Imagine being taught to be afraid of something that should be sacred.

I believed that if I went to confession, then my sins would be forgiven, and I'd have a better chance of making it to Heaven. I never felt comfortable telling someone my sins, especially someone I didn't even know. The first time I ever walked into a confessional, I was around seven years old. I remember because it was dark, and I felt claustrophobic. I hesitated at first but didn't really feel like I had a choice, and everyone else seemed to be doing it. Besides, I wanted to go to Heaven one day. As I got older, I began to question everything about religion, the church, and God as well.

I didn't really understand the concept of death at that time, because no one had died that I was close to until I was in my early teens when my grandfather passed away. It was a very painful time for me, and I remember feeling so scared. It was the first time

I ever experienced death, and the one thing I knew for sure was that I didn't want to die. That deep fear of death stayed with me until much later in my life. There were times when I use to lay in bed at night terrified that if I closed my eyes, I might not wake up in the morning. I would eventually just cry myself to sleep. I struggled with the idea of dying for years. It robbed me of my ability to thoroughly enjoy life. I was so afraid of dying and losing my loved ones that it started to take over my life. I was constantly worried to the point where I felt out of control.

Fear and worry shaped my life and became my reality.

I was afraid of dying, of not being good enough, of making wrong decisions, and expressing myself. I began to doubt myself and was never happy with who I was. I felt intimidated by others, especially by people I didn't know. I never felt smart enough or pretty enough. I could see these things in others, but failed to see them in myself. There were times when I felt like I was drowning in my own tears.

I had married when I was nineteen and was blessed with two beautiful daughters by the time I was twenty-four. I was young and very insecure at the time. All of the fears that I had been feeling got worse as time went on, and my relationship became more and more abusive.

I left the church in my early thirties after an altercation I had involving my eldest daughter. She had been born with a developmental delay and wasn't able to learn the prayers that were necessary for her to receive her confirmation, a ceremony that all Catholic children go through.

Because of her delay and inability to memorize the prayers, they refused to let her be confirmed.

I will never forget the feelings that I was left with from that experience. I was angry and felt totally betrayed by the church. I questioned their decision, and they couldn't give me any other answer other than she was incapable of saying the prayers. I asked if anyone could assist her through it, and they said that it wasn't something they allowed, and she would need to do it on her own.

I felt this sudden disappointment rise up inside of me as I looked at my daughter's face. She had been bullied enough already, and I remember thinking, *This is the house of God? Is this what God would say or do?* I took my daughter's hand, and I left knowing that I was never going back.

I was really struggling at the time with so much of my life. My relationship wasn't getting any better, and it felt like my life was falling apart. I didn't know what to do. My insecurities were there to remind me that I wasn't good enough or smart enough to do it on my own.

A couple of years later, I began my personal growth journey. I felt a strong need to move forward in my life, and I was hoping that I could find some answers. I have to say that at first, I experienced a lot of resistance towards what I was learning. I somehow felt it wasn't possible for me to achieve my dreams and goals. All of those fears were still inside of me, just waiting for the opportunity to surface. You can't do that. You aren't good enough. You don't have what it takes.

I spent the next four years delving into anything that involved personal growth. I believe this was the beginning of what I call my spiritual awakening. Whether it was reading books, or going to seminars or workshops, I did it. I was hooked. I began to feel different as time went on. I noticed that some of my fears lessened, and that I was more motivated and excited about life. I didn't feel like I would cry at the drop of a hat and physically, I felt stronger. I suddenly felt hopeful that this was what I was looking for. That this awakening would fill the missing piece inside of me.

I finally worked up the courage to leave my eighteen-year-old marriage behind, and a year later I found my soulmate, whom I later married and created a beautiful life with.

One day I was sitting at my desk at work, thinking that I needed to go and get another book before going home for the day. I had been reading a lot and continued to try and make sense of my life. After work, I went to the nearby second-hand bookstore. As I was strolling through the store and searching through the shelves, I suddenly remembered a book that a friend of mine had recommended called *Return to Love* by Marianne Williamson.

I asked the store owner if they had it in stock, and the lady directed me to where it was on the shelves. As I reached for the book, I remember feeling butterflies running through my whole body. I'd had butterflies in my stomach before, but never throughout my whole body. I took a step back, wondering what was going on. After a few moments, the feeling subsided, and I proceeded to the checkout to pay for the book.

The owner looked at me, and with a tear in her eye, she said, "This book changed my life."

When I got home, I began reading. As I turned the pages, my body quivered, and my eyes began to well up. I could feel the tears flowing down my cheeks, and my hands were trembling. I never experienced anything like this before. Something inside of me was changing, and I knew it. I felt it!

The words, "love is the power" ran deeply within me. I kept hearing them over and over and over again, like a broken record. What did all of this mean? No book had ever affected me this way before.

Return to Love taught me how love was the solution and answer to all of our problems. That we came from love and will always return to love. It helped me to see that there is no Hell; there's only Heaven and that God is good and judges no one.

As I read further, I began to understand just how powerful love is and how my fears had been overpowering the love that I hold within me. It helped me to see parts of myself that I had never seen before. I now understood that God is love and there is no judgment where love exists. This was one of the most profound messages that I was ever given because it changed everything that I had come to believe. I felt alive again. This is what I always knew that I hadn't yet discovered, until now. This was the missing piece inside of me!

Upon finishing the book, I felt this overwhelming feeling of joy overcome me. For the first time, I felt I had my life back.

I suddenly realized that there was so much more to life than what I'd been experiencing. I had spent so many years being afraid, but somehow, I felt that I no longer had to live with those fears. I knew that the religious path I was on was not one that symbolized love, but one that constituted fear.

It hasn't been an easy journey as my ego is still insistent on bringing up those fears. However, I started to feel an inner peace and calmness that I hadn't experienced before. The more I studied and became aware of who I was, the more things began shifting in a big way.

I can now experience fear without resistance, and I'm able to move through it. I no longer fear death. I see it not as an end, but as a gift, a new journey for my soul.

I no longer resist what I feel. I now know if I have a belief that doesn't feel good or right, I can shift that belief to what feels right for me. I've learned to let go of fear-based beliefs and then choose a new belief to focus on that's loving and nurturing. I know through my years of experience that when you are connected and in a state of love, there is nothing that can't be healed and transformed.

Just a year ago I was diagnosed with COPD, apparently caused by smoking when I was younger. I had been experiencing a feeling in my chest that I can't quite explain. When it wasn't going away, I decided to see my doctor who sent me for a chest x-ray. When the doctor told me the results, I was in shock. I had always been very healthy, so this wasn't at all what I was expecting. I suddenly felt anxious, and the fear started to move through my body. What I noticed was that this fear that I was experiencing wasn't a fear of dying, which at one time in my life it certainly would have been. This was a fear that I might have to change certain things in my life. What was I going to do?

Before leaving his office, my doctor scheduled another x-ray as well as an EKG and pulmonary breathing test, which I was to have done in a month's time. On my way home, I started thinking about how I could change my situation. One of the most valuable lessons I've learned and come to believe through this journey is that anything is possible, and it's our own limitations that hold us back and keep us from healing and transforming our experiences.

From that day and for the next three weeks, I would begin my healing process. I spent twenty minutes twice a day working with my body. My intention was to heal my body before having my next tests. I would connect to my body and then breathe while bringing love into my chest area. After a couple of weeks, I could already feel the difference. I continued the process for another week before the feeling I had been experiencing was completely gone.

A week later I went for my tests. First my EKG, then my pulmonary breathing test and finally, the x-ray. I then had the anticipation of waiting to get the results. The following week I returned to the doctors. No signs of COPD. I have been back for a six-month and yearly x-ray, and there are still no signs of COPD. The doctor didn't understand how it could just disappear, as there is no cure. This is the kind of miracle that can occur when we are in a state of love.

My experience has been such a gift. I have examined my beliefs and realized that most of them aren't really mine, but are those of others, or society itself. I know now that what I believe becomes my reality, and what I experience in my life is the result of those beliefs.

We have the ability to sense our feelings, yet we often ignore them. The religious beliefs that I was holding onto all of those years no longer exist. I know that God is within me. I still pray every night, but I'm no longer praying to a being outside of me, I'm praying to a higher intelligence within me. I can't always see it, but I know it's there.

I have learned that there are so many choices, so many possibilities that I now have access to by allowing my feelings to guide me.

I've gained a sense of peace and confidence that helps me to express myself more rather than holding everything inside. I feel good about who I am. I've learned to love myself for all that I am.

I have learned that before I make a choice, I need to ask myself what is it that I truly believe and what am I really afraid of. I listen, and I feel what's happening inside of me.

At first, I found it so hard to understand that God wasn't out there. That the person I was praying to didn't exist as someone, but as something. Something that is within me—that is within all of us. I couldn't grasp the idea that we are all one. That we are one with God, Spirit, Source, the Universe or whatever name you give to that higher intelligence. That we aren't separate from anyone or anything.

This is what has changed my life. I can see that we are mirrors for everyone and everything around us. I now live my life knowing that I'm okay. Feeling that I am enough, worthy, and deserving. Feeling confident in my choices and decisions. Knowing that when any given situation or challenge occurs, it's okay to let it take its course rather than try to control it or fight against it. At the end of it, there is something greater than we can ever imagine.

Every day is a new adventure with new opportunities, new challenges, and precious moments.

Today, what I was once afraid of and what I once struggled with has empowered me to take charge of my life and to help others do the same.

Overcoming your fears by returning to love allows you to shine your light on the world and be the powerful being that you truly are!

Marija Strât

Marija has a Master of Behavioral Science and education in psychotherapy. Her field of expertise is energy psychology.

Marija is the founder of Re-Member, an all-inclusive healing modality. Her deep commitment to life has taken healing beyond time and space, and includes her client's ancestors, previous lifetimes and other dimensions. She has more than fifteen years' experience of facilitating healing for people globally.

Marija appreciates life to the fullest and lives in Contagious Flow as a natural part of everyday life. She openheartedly speaks Light Language, a method of speaking and singing that connects us to our heart. As often as possible, Marija walks barefooted to be in direct contact with the earth.

Find Marija online:

www.re-member.one
www.iamthepath.com
www.iamthepath.se

Emotions – The Colors of Life

By Marija Stråt

Over the past few days, it was harder and harder to breathe. I could hear the sound of pipes when I was taking a breath. It was so heavy to breathe, so much effort put in every breath. I could feel the restriction – there was not enough room in my lungs for the air that I needed.

Usually, I would just take my inhaler, and relief would come in a minute or two. It had always worked— until now. I had already taken medicine three times that day, and it was not even noon yet. I was getting worried and felt the panic rise.

I couldn't understand what was going on. I had never been in a situation like this before. I hadn't been close to anything I was allergic to. In fact, I had been home for two weeks. The doctor had given me sick leave for a month due to fatigue.

I knew I could have unexpected asthma when I was at work, or at a friend's house. A single hair from a cat or a dog could be enough to start an allergic reaction. The smell of horses or horse hair had shown to be life-threatening to me. So, I kept away from animals—and people. Animal hair on someone's clothing was enough to make me sick.

It had been like this for about twenty-five years. I had gotten used to living a restricted life. It was just the way it was. I could only visit people who did not have any animals, and these were the only people that could visit me. I avoided the movies. I seldom went by train or bus – I limited my exposure to the public. Admittedly, it was a lonely life, but at least I could breathe, and that was the most important thing.

That day I had an appointment for a massage. It was not a habit of mine. I had only treated myself to massages a few times before. During the massage, I mentioned how bothered I was with my breathing. While enjoying the massage, I started to drift away, as the masseuse talked to me with her soft voice. She said, "That's your body talking. All bodies do that. Physical issues are the body's way of trying to get your attention. The body wants you to listen to it. It has an important message for you."

During the early hours of the next morning, the masseuse's words came back to me: 'the body has something to say to me'. I was puzzled. She had mentioned something about the connection between body and mind. Could they be connected? Would the body deliver messages from the mind? Why would it do that? It was so confusing... I drifted off to sleep again.

Message to you from your body. The words kept popping up while I prepared breakfast. I could hear my children starting to put their things together for school before they came out to join me in the kitchen.

"Are you all set? Have you brought a change of clothing and a towel for gymnastics?" I asked my son.

"My towel is still wet," he replied. "It's still wet from last time."

I could feel my breathing becoming restricted. "Haven't you put it on the clothesline to dry? Has it been in your gymnastic bag for several days?"

I started to cough and reached for my medicine. Then I remembered, *My body speaks to me. What message does it have? I* listened, and I felt... nothing...I couldn't feel anything special.

Okay, I thought to myself, *the breathing got restricted some minutes ago. What happened then?* In my mind's eye, I went back to the conversation with my son. I had to look at it a few times before I realized what it was about.

I noticed my emotional response was missing. If it had happened to someone else, the emotional response could have been anger.

"I am angry," I said.

I tried, "I am angry" a few more times.

"I am angry. I am angry. I am angry."

Something was still missing.

"I am angry, AND I can breathe." It felt good to say that!

Later the same day, I could hear the wheeze from my breath and felt the heaviness again. *What would the message be now?* I looked at my situation. I could see I was busy. I was in the middle of organizing my papers, paying bills and had promised to run an errand for my dad before 2 pm.

"What would my state of mind be in this situation?" I mumbled to myself. I gave it some thought before I found the words.

"I am stressed out, AND I can breathe."

I wasn't actually stressed, but I thought it would be a normal feeling in a situation like this.

I was surprised when, a few minutes later when my wheezing stopped. The air was not completely flowing, but breathing was easier. Could this be the key?

For the next few weeks, every time I felt it was difficult to breathe, I did the same thing. I looked at the situation as an observer, and I used logic to figure out the message. I said it out loud with the ending, "…AND I can breathe."

I am sad, AND I can breathe.

I don't want to do this, AND I can breathe.

I feel neglected, AND I can breathe.

It worked every time!

The process of transformation was interesting. Direct contact with the emotions was not needed for the healing to take place. It was enough that my intellect translated my body's message. And then I said the message out loud.

It only took a month to be free of asthma when I was in an allergy free environment. What a relief.

A couple of months later, I was actually starting to feel the emotions that my logical mind had figured out.

The Gift of Life

The emotional root cause of my asthma came from a series of traumatic events in my childhood when my mother was very ill. Back then, the only way I knew how to handle emotions was to suppress them.

When I was eleven, my mother suddenly died, and I started to cry. On the second day, my father looked at me and told me I had to stop crying. Anyone who knew my father at that time knew this was not a suggestion, but an order. I stopped crying immediately.

As an adult, I understand that my father couldn't deal with his own emotions, so my tears made him uncomfortable. I believed I had to stop crying, otherwise, my father would leave me.

Asthma restricted what I could do and was sometimes a real threat to my life. When I consciously understood that my body was talking to me, and when I started to translate the messages, eventually I came into direct contact with my emotions. The asthma was no longer needed because I was no longer suppressing my emotions.

Asthma was a precious gift that brought me full access to my emotions and by that, a more colorful and happy life.

Finding Peace

One Wednesday afternoon a few years later, the phone rang. A man called and introduced himself as a police officer. He asked if I could come by for a meeting. *What a wonderful opportunity*, I thought excitedly. *The police are interested in working with me.* I had been on the lookout for projects I could do with larger companies.

"Do you have any clue why you are here?" the policeman asked when we met. "I suppose your daughter has already told you."

Thoughts started to spin in my head. *My daughter? What's her connection to this project?* I was confused. Then I realized the meeting couldn't be about a joint project.

"What has happened to my daughter?" I asked, with worry in my voice.

My breathing had become shallow, and my heart raced. I leaned forward. "What has happened? Is she in any danger?"

The policeman looked a bit surprised. "Hasn't she called you?"

No, I hadn't talked to my daughter for weeks. I was confused. My head was full of questions. *Why am I here? What is the matter with my daughter?*

"Until recently she lived in an apartment that I owned. She wanted to move in with her boyfriend. I put the apartment up for sale, but my daughter was upset because it did not go smoothly. Eventually, she had stopped answering my phone calls. She didn't reply to text messages. I haven't talked to her, and she hasn't called me," I said frantically. "What is this all about?" I asked, wanting to put some order into the situation.

The policeman looked at me from the other side of the table. "She says she has been molested."

I immediately remembered a conversation I had with her a few years earlier. It was about a job offer she got from the small local restaurant. I had a bad feeling about it. It made no sense for the owner to hire her when business was slow.

The slurping sound when the policeman took a sip of his coffee drew me back to the present moment at the police station. "Did he harm her?" I asked. "Did the restaurant owner hurt her?"

"She has not said anything about a restaurant owner," he replied. "She says *you* have molested her."

In an instant, the world stopped. I was totally blank. There were no thoughts, no emotions. I couldn't feel my body any longer.

The policeman continued to slurp his coffee. For him, this was just an ordinary day at work. For me, the world had just turned upside down. I had nothing to hold on to any longer.

"She filed a police complaint that you have molested her, several times. The police complaint is about you," he said, after what seemed like an age.

My daughter accusing me of molesting her!? I can't make any sense of this. It felt like the wiring in my brain disconnected. I am totally confused. I don't understand what's going on. Is this really happening to me? Is it a mistake? Could the policeman have mixed up the reports with someone else's?

The policeman looked me straight into the eyes and asked, "Have you molested your daughter?"

"No, I haven't," I heard myself saying.

When I walked away from the police station, I could feel my legs and hands shaking. I had trouble getting the car keys out of my pocket. I leaned against the car. Breathing. My legs would not hold my weight for much longer. I managed to open the car and sit in the driver's seat. Now my whole body was shaking, and tears came from my eyes. *What just happened? What am I in the middle of?*

I knew I was in shock. To calm my body, I focused on my breathing, to make it deeper and slower. Eventually, I drove back home. I needed space to just be, to be nurtured with safe surroundings.

While pouring myself some tea, I looked at the cup's yellow flowers against the turquoise background. The beauty of the cup usually made me smile, but not today. I felt distant from all my emotions.

I could use this emotion-free space to see what was best for me. I knew the outcome if I didn't take care of myself emotionally in this stressful situation. When you experience trauma and emotions are suppressed, normal everyday life will be deeply affected. I would experience more fear and worry, most likely on a daily basis. It would be hard to relax, so my sleep would be negatively impacted. Nightmares would come. The risk of physical illnesses would increase due to the high levels of stress in my body.

I knew this was what I was facing if I neglected to process what I had just experienced. Trauma in my childhood had shown me the hard way what the consequences were. I have had post-traumatic stress since before my teens. My allergies started then as well, and more allergies were added as I grew older. Further physical challenges had come over the years, including severe asthma, IBS, aching muscles, stiff joints, and far-reaching fatigue.

As an adult, I had the opportunity to really explore and investigate the nature of emotions. Both during the many hours I spent in healing my own childhood traumas and also as a witness when my clients were going through an emotional detox in psychotherapy.

I know emotions well. I understand them and how they act. They are very predictable. Emotions have a natural flow. They peak, then they subside. Eventually, they fade away completely, and only harmony remains.

I could see that life had prepared me well for the challenging situation I was in now. Trauma release was one of my specialties.

I knew it would not be pleasant to go through the emotions of the situation at hand, but when completed, it would be very healing for my body, mind, and spirit.

I choose two important pieces to begin with:

1. Talk about what happened with people I feel safe with – don't make it a secret.

2. Let the emotions have their natural flow.

I told my closest family members. My heart started to pound in my chest when I picked up the phone to call my father. I could feel my hands turning wet, and I got uncomfortably sweaty under my arms. I could hear my thoughts, *What would people say if they knew? What would my father say?* This was not a pleasant situation at all. I really wanted to just hide and forget about the meeting at the police station. Nevertheless, I took a deep breath and continued.

I also called my siblings. Just to inform them about the situation at hand. I could feel I was still in the state of shock. It was easy to leave the emotions out of the story. I talked about everything like it happened to someone else.

I was so surprised how well they all handled it. No blame or shame from their side. Just a willingness to understand. Talking about how memories are created, and how false memories can emerge. They were able to embrace both me and my daughter. They didn't want to exclude either of us. What a relief. I could feel my shoulders relaxing and my breathing slowing down. We had the support of solving this in a loving way.

Now came the next piece, to let the emotions have their natural movement, so they could return to harmony.

I closed my eyes to connect more fully to my body, and I began tapping on the meridian points. I was used to tapping as a good method for getting clients in contact with their suppressed emotions. Soon I felt that my body started to tremble. Fear was coming up big time. I was in survival mode. *How would I survive? I was facing prison. What would happen to me? To my life?*

The fear started to subside, and instead, sadness rose up. Tears started to run down my cheeks. *How can I prove my innocence? What if they don't believe me?*

The sadness was overtaken by shame. I just wanted to hide. I curled up in the corner of my armchair, putting my arms over my head, not wanted to be seen. *What if anyone hears what I have been accused of? What if they think I molested my daughter?*

I felt despondent, as if there was no hope. That It would be better if I killed myself. I pictured a rope around my neck. My breathing was heavy. I felt pressure in my head.

It would be best for everyone if I didn't exist any longer. I felt I had no value. I was a total failure. This was really uncomfortable. I started to tap more frequently on the energy points to make the emotion transform quicker.

Finally, I could feel the despondency subsiding. I stretched my arms and legs that had been curled up during the process. I reached for the teacup. The tea was cold, and I looked at the clock. I had been releasing emotions for an hour.

I reflected upon the emotional process that was taking place. The emotions moved like waves. They peaked and then subsided. This was the natural flow. I knew I was in a healing process.

I closed my eyes again and got in touch with how stiff and sore my body was, like I'd been in a battle. Then I felt it. I was so angry – holy Moses! I stood up and shouted, "How dare you!" I allowed the raw anger inside me to rise. Suppressing my emotions was not an option. I heard myself blaming her.

"What the hell have you done?! I am so disappointed in you!"

I knew that this too was a natural part of the process. For the healing to be complete, nothing could be censured. I let everything out, exactly as it wanted to be expressed.

I knew that healing is, by nature, quite a quick process. So, over the next days, I made room for the process to continue. On the fourth day, I noticed that the intensity of the emotions had subsided considerably. I could think and do other things, without this being on my mind. I slept well at night.

The Happy Ending

We long for the happy endings in movies and books. We feel at peace when everything turns out well in the end. In an attempt to create this in our own lives, we turn ourselves inside-out to make our close ones happy and to put things in order for everyone. When challenges arise, we notice that the peace slip away. We have such a longing for peace, that's why we keep on trying to create it in our surroundings, over and over again. Thinking that peace has to do with the people and situations around us.

But it doesn't. The opposite is actually true. Peace comes from within. From within you.

You could easily think, that being a peaceful person all the time, will only be possible if you come from a very loving and supportive upbringing and have a smooth and perfect life.

Well, I'm happy to say, it doesn't. Peace has nothing to do with perfection. I know that from my own life and from witnessing several hundreds of my client's stories. You have now read two of my stories and can see that my peace does not come from having perfect circumstances around me.

You may wonder what happened to the police complaint. It was dropped a couple of months later. It is now ten years since the hearing at the police station, and I haven't talked to my daughter since. She decided she didn't want to have any contact with me.

This could have been a disaster for me as a mother. Instead, I chose to do detox emotionally on everything that was triggered, so the wounds would heal. The transformation that took place was truly magical. I have opened up to a peace that is beyond my imagination. This peace comes from inside of me. Over the years since then, I've encountered so much peace that I literally bathe in it.

It turned out that my daughter has been the perfect teacher for me to find lasting peace. She has shown me that I was looking in the wrong direction, searching for it in situations around me. She has opened up new doors for me, to see, that peace comes from my deep connection to myself. The connection to my essence. I now live life naturally in touch with my true essence.

It is the same with you. When you connect to yourself, on that deep level, you come in contact with your inner peace. Peace is a flavor of your essence. It is who you are. I think you know what I am talking about. Maybe you have experienced it when singing, playing music, painting, dancing, being in meditation or yoga, looking at the stars, being in nature, with animals or looking into the eyes of a newborn child.

So why don't you experience peace all the time? That is because it's easy to be distracted when challenges arise. Challenges arise as a natural part of life. They happen for everyone, and you can't prevent them.

What you can do is to move through the challenges and come out of them, being empowered — living your life more aligned with your essence, feeling more peaceful and being in love with yourself and life.

The first key is to this is to *know who you are*. When you know your essence, it is easy to distinguish between when you are in contact with your essence or when in contact with something else.

The second is to *notice* when you are not in contact with yourself.

The third is to know *how to bring yourself back* to your essence. It can be with techniques like EFT tapping and Re-Member healing, which helps the emotions to transform. Meditation or yoga usually stops the mind chatter, and being in nature also calms the mind.

The fourth is to *act on it*, to actually bring yourself back. Learn helpful techniques that you can use on a daily basis, and when you're facing challenges. Remember that it's usually all about emotions. Let the emotions go through their natural healing process. Have the support that you need. When going through very intense emotions, it's usually best to have the support from a therapist. When possible, let the process begin immediately.

Turning emotions into harmony is one of the most precious gifts I have. With this, in a very short period of time, I can turn life challenges into something that empowers me, and I continue to be filled with even more peace than ever before.

So can you. I wish you all the best!

Inga Thengils

Ingibjorg R Thengilsdottir, or Inga Thengils as she is known outside of Iceland, is an international spiritual channeler who has inspired thousands of people to connect with their heart and their spiritual guides.

Inga started her journey in 1990 and trained with medium Terry Evans for five years. She has trained in homeopathy, Reiki healing, and is certified as a yoga teacher with Shanti Desai.

Inga believes that self-care and support starts at home. She connects to her heart, and it is from this place that she supports her clients.

Find Inga online:

www.themiraclemessenger.com
https://twitter.com/miraclemessenge
https://www.facebook.com/themiraclemessenger/

From Resistance to Spiritual Power

By Inga Thengils

It all started when I was born, in a village on the east coast of Iceland, in the autumn of 1957, on a stormy winter night. My mother was brought to the hospital by a rescue team. They had to carry her, as no car could drive due to the snow that was covering the roads. Thankfully, it was a short distance.

I was born at 1 am that morning. I was big, so my mother struggled a lot and was very tired after the birth. I was taken out of the room and stayed with the midwife until the next morning. I was then brought to my mother in a beautiful dress with a bow in my hair. The midwife that was holding me said, "She is so beautiful with her mass of black hair and big, bright eyes that I have been cuddling her the whole night. I could not resist dressing her up." With these words, she handed me over to my mother.

Ever since, I have felt this event describes the story of my life. My life has been difficult in so many ways, but there have always been people that have seen me for who I really am and acknowledged my strength and beauty.

One evening, when I was four years old, my mother put me to bed. I was not allowed to have the light on, and I was so scared of the dark. I was convinced there was a creature in the closet that no one seemed to know about except me. I was crying softly into my pillow when suddenly, I heard a sound—I heard music. I stopped crying and looked up to see lights on my ceiling. I instantly sat up, thinking that my mother must have brought my dad's flashlight. I looked around, but there was no one there except me and this dancing light on the ceiling. I lay down and heard soothing voices that said, "Dear sweet Inga,you are safe. Go to sleep, we will look out for you." And instantly, I fell asleep.

I lived with my parents and the maternal side of my family in this village until I was nine years old. They were good years. I had a lot of support from my grandmother Anna, who often told me tales of elves, trolls, and hidden people. She also taught me how powerful dreams are, and how important it is to remember them. Her stories made so much sense to me because I knew they where true. How did I know that? I saw these creatures all the time.

I saw spirits of nature, the goddesses in the mountains, little flower elves, the spirit of the rivers, the power in the fog. Even bad weather, like a snowstorm, has a spirit.

It was then that my parents decided to move away from this peaceful place to a bigger town where there were more employment opportunities for my father. It all happened very quickly, and we had only a very few short months to get used to the idea.

I looked forward to the move, and getting to know my father's family. At the same time, I remember there was a constant heavy feeling in my stomach. I did not know why, but I would soon find out. It was difficult to leave everything that I loved so deeply, but leaving my grandmother was heartbreaking. I remember that I did not want to say goodbye to her when we left, as I had a feeling I would not see her anytime soon. Traveling was not easy for her, and my grandmother hated to speak on the phone.

My family and I moved into a very nice house, and I really liked it. It was brand new and in a neighborhood that was filled with young families with children. It looked perfect, or so I thought.

My dreams and hopes for this new adventure were very quickly shattered. When I started at my new school, I was a happy nine-year-old girl. When I left that school three years later, nothing of that girl remained.

I was a wreck after three years of constant bullying, but I never dared to open up and tell my story. I shut down and closed myself off from everyone, and everything. I became a depressed, sad version of myself. In those days, no one spoke of bullying and its effects. Those that experienced it were left full of shame and self-loathing, because it had to be their fault. That is exactly how I felt.

I continued my journey, closed up and felt a lot of resistance within myself on all levels. I carried so much fear that I was always tired, out of focus, and had no self-esteem.

I carried this devotion to resistance through my first marriage— unhappy and broken. It was really no surprise that it ended in divorce, as we were both very young. I really used my first marriage as an excuse to get away from my life, even though that's not what actually happened.

In August 1985, I met my second husband Jon, and we are still happily married. We instantly connected because we had similar interests. We both like dancing, traveling and spending time with friends and family.

Jon's past was very different from mine, but we had one thing in common. We both had been hurt and had issues that we needed to work through. However, he took the time to grow and heal, whereas I was still resisting.

The first few years of our marriage were difficult, but Jon was always there for me, always looking for ways to help me. But I was so stuck in my head that nothing worked. I continued to reject myself, afraid of stepping away from my zone of resistance. I never ever connected with my heart; that was just too scary.

As I am writing this, I know why I never cried, not even one tear in all these years. You cannot cry when you are stuck in your head all the time, and even today it is still hard for me to shed tears.

Jon wanted to introduce me to spiritual life, feeling that it might help me. He came up with the idea of reading spiritual books. I started with *Messages from Michel* by Chelsea Quinn Yarbro. I loved reading because I did not have to leave my head to be able to embrace the content and allow the words to support me. This led to me wanting to learn more.

One day, a friend told me about a meditation group. I was very curious, and even a little excited. So, we went to a group weekend seminar, and I learned to meditate. It was then that I discovered I had a spectacular intuitiveness and the ability to channel from other realms.

I was able to channel, meditate and be very sensitive to other people's needs. I realized how much I loved helping people in this way. As I learned more, I recognized that I was—and sometimes still am—two different people (the spiritual channeler and Inga Thengils). I know this might sound really strange, but it took me years to realize that these two people were alive within me and merge them together.

I was a very successful spiritual channeler in Iceland and Europe for many years, but that sad, heavy feeling still lingered inside me.

I was constantly spending time and money looking for help and support.

During one of these searches for support, I decided I would like to have a child. Over a ten year period, I had three miscarriages and three IVF treatments. When I was forty years old, and on my fourth IVF treatment, I finally became pregnant and gave birth to my youngest son in 1998. I should have been elated; even though I loved my boy dearly, I was still stuck in my resistance zone. I didn't know how to be happy.

Over the next few years, I threw myself into taking care of my son and working with my husband Jon on our joint business. My husband is an electrician and specializes in handling automation for all kinds of doors. The business is very successful and supported us completely. I feel that was one of the reasons why I stopped my channeling business; I felt that neither my business or me were good enough.

I did not stop my search for happiness. I was constantly aware of this nagging feeling inside of me that something was not right, that there must be something more. I kept believing that the next seminar would be the one to fix my problems. But nothing worked. My sweet husband said so many times, "My dear Inga, I love you, but I cannot help you if you are not willing to help yourself. " Yet, I continued to stay where I was, because at the time it seemed easier.

In my search for a solution, I trained as a homeopath, a yoga teacher, a Reiki healer, and more. All of this was helpful, in a way—at least my body was healthy and strong.

After my graduation in homeopathy in 2009, I thought that was to be my life's work. I told myself I was happy, but I wasn't. It had become very difficult for me to listen to my clients' stories. Their illnesses and struggles affected me deeply.

Believing this was what I was born to do, I continued to uplevel myself as a homeopath and came across the opportunity to go to a conference in Copenhagen in September 2011. A friend of mine and I decided to go together.

When we arrived after an uneventful flight, we decided to do some grocery shopping. When we were leaving the shop, I tripped over a plastic plate on the floor that was used to display furniture. As I fell, I heard a voice inside me say, *Inga! When are you going to listen?* I thought, *Oh shit, did this accident really have to happen so I would listen?* I knew I had blacked out, and that something was happening that I had no control over. I knew that I *had* to follow the voice that I felt was still inside of me. I decided to answer and said, *I will listen, but you must help me to get home. To find the best doctor to help me heal so I can continue to listen and find out what it is that you want to tell me. Please do this for me.*

Instantly, the pain from the fall lessened so that I could handle it better. I was taken to the hospital where I was told by a doctor that I had broken my right arm, dislocated my right shoulder, had a slight concussion, and a swollen right knee. All they could do was bandage me up and send me home with my x-rays.

Throughout this process, I was constantly aware of the help and support from my spiritual guides. I could feel their presence and heard how gently they spoke to me to remind me to keep my promise.

This was when I finally started my journey of healing and change.

That evening when I came back to the apartment after being in the hospital, I phoned the airlines and changed my ticket to get back home as soon as possible. There was a seat available on one airplane, so I took it. I ordered a wheelchair service for the airport, and then I went to bed. The funny thing is that I slept so peacefully even though I'd had such a hectic experience.

The next day at the airport I noticed that everyone was smiling at me and asking if I needed anything, or if they could help me in any way. On the plane, a very nice gentleman took care of me all the way home. He gave me a snack that he had with him (I couldn't manage a knife and fork due to my dislocation), put on my headset and found a movie for me to watch while he arranged my pillows and blanket. He even held my unbroken hand when we were landing in Iceland, and he stayed with me until someone came to take me in a wheelchair to meet my husband.

I know now that these people were angels in the form of humans that were sent by my spiritual guides to help me. I believe this because I have had so much proof that angels do exist. I believe in them.

At home, the first thing I did was call the hospital. They told me that because I was injected with a needle in the ambulance in Copenhagen, I had to have a special test to make sure I didn't bring any bacteria into my local hospital.

I had to wait eight days for the test results! I stayed home, but the strange thing was, I had hardly any pain. I could sleep, and I could walk. It was impossible to move the dislocated arm, so they were challenging days. Have you ever tried to put a leash on a seven-month-old puppy with one arm? It wasn't easy, but I managed it! I remembered the promise from my guides and told myself that I'd be okay.

Finally, my operation day came, and I went to the hospital.

While I was waiting to be seen, a man in white robes came into my room and sat on my bed. My first thought was that he was some kind of a therapist or a social worker that was there to talk to me about the operation. I was very surprised when he introduced himself and said, "I am here to save your arm. " Then he gently put his hand on me and said, "Do not worry, I am the best orthopedic doctor in Iceland. I will fix everything, and you will be just fine. " I instantly relaxed and trusted this man. Of course, he was one more angel to take care of me, just as my spiritual guides had promised.

The operation went well, and I stayed in the hospital for two nights. On the morning of the third day, I went home. I could not do much, so I had plenty of time to contemplate what had happened and what would come next.

First of all, I wanted to know more about my spiritual guides and decided that that would be my first step. It came crystal clear to me that conversation was not enough; more was needed from me. I made a huge commitment to open my heart, something that was very difficult for me.

Thankfully my healing was quick. When I went for a checkup one month later, my doctor said, "I have never seen such quick healing in a person in their fifties before."

He then asked, "What did you do? "

I said, "I prayed, and I knew that I was going to be fine. "

"Wow," he said. "Can you pray for me too? "

I said, "Yes, of course, I will pray for you," and thanked him for his help.

This made me more confident in owning my promise. I started a new life where I was always guided gently back to my heart whenever I forgot my promise and shifted back into my resistance zone.

I truly believe that every journey has a purpose and every step you take on that journey has a purpose. You will know when you are taking the right steps because the signs will be there. You just need to listen for them.

Today I channel and mentor my clients that have had similar experiences with spiritual guides, but are struggling with how to handle those experiences. I take them on a journey to connect with themselves and their spiritual guides.

Our spiritual guides are truly remarkable. They can do anything for us, we just need to reach out and ask.

My dream is to stay on the path of creativity and curiosity. To never give up and always move forward. This is my wish for you, the reader, as well.

Wendy Yellen

Wendy Yellen has received the International Top Three Transformational Experts Award in her field, every year for the past decade. She lives near Santa Fe, New Mexico near the top of a 7,200-foot-high mesa, with her husband and partner of over forty years, Michael.

Wendy graduated from Brandeis University and received her Master's in Social Work from Smith College. She later studied and was certified in emotional release body work and numerous traditional and non-traditional forms of healing from masters around the world. However, Wendy let all of these go once she discovered the power of the ancient art and 21st-century science, Eidetics.

Find Wendy online:

www.MySpiritualManifesto.com

Illusion, Delusion, and the Emerging Lotus

By Wendy Yellen

How did I—a fifty-something world traveler and respected therapist—end up in this double-wide trailer, yelling, for the first time *in my life* at my father? It wasn't pretty, but it woke me up to a shift that mattered.

I'm horrified at myself. How in the world did I ever get here? Me? Shocking myself with who I am being. I'm lost. I'm terrified. And I don't know how to get out of it.

Let's go back in time, to Houston Texas in the 1980's. Backed by degrees and training in traditional and non-traditional therapies, a Master's of Social Work from Smith College School for Social Work and a Family Therapy Fellowship, I opened a private practice that seemed to successfully boom all by itself.

I ran a full practice. I had 100% referral/word-of-mouth clients, a waiting list, and six-week adventurous vacations each year. I was saving money so easily that I didn't even feel it. Unlike some of my colleagues, I didn't cram my practice with forty client hours a week, which felt crazy to me. I paid attention to what really worked for ME, for the lifestyle that I wanted, which was simple, clean, and easy. My clients loved working with me, so much so that they referred *their* friends and *their* clients. I had no idea how 'lucky' I was because this full practice flowed gently to me like a clean, clear, sparkling brook. But it streamed towards me so naturally in part because I was paying attention to who I was being, and how that made me feel.

I loved working with clients to make real changes in their lives. Many had been sexually abused as children, and the traditional and non-traditional processes I used seemed perfect because the work was in the head *and* in the body. I had noticed that when people—including me—were only coming from their head, the work was stilted, shallow, and less effective.

And yet, something was off. I wasn't burned out, and I still *loved* my work. But pulling back the lens, now, years later, I can see that I must have known, on some level, that something was off. Deep inside me, I knew that there MUST be more effective ways to help people REALLY change. And even if my clients were thrilled with their progress, I knew, I hoped, that there HAD to be more effective ways to transform.

Then, an opportunity came for my husband Michael and me to move to Japan so he could study aikido and other Japanese martial arts. We took it. Crazy? Maybe. But years before, I had spent three years on my own traveling in Europe and Israel, and I loved living in foreign countries, learning new languages and absorbing different perspectives that forced me to reconsider what I *thought* was 'normal'.

After five years living together in Japan, I felt like I *had* to return to the US, as if living away were a kind of hiatus on life, and I needed to get back to my life, back to making a difference.

When I got back, I didn't reopen my practice. I simply refused. I was no longer willing to do transformational work, even with all the excellent tools I had, if change was *this* superficial. My clients didn't think it was superficial, but I knew in my cells that there MUST be more. Closing my practice completely and not working as a therapist seemed crazy to all the people who loved me—even the woman who cut my hair shook her head in disbelief. My sister was confused too. "Wendy, you *are* a therapist, it's in your DNA, I can feel it. How can you *not* do it?" she would ask me. But I refused.

Conventional 'wisdom' says if you are successful—especially financially—don't stop! But, I have to *love* what I do, and I have to *know* it's making a difference, which to me, is even more important than the money. Of course I absolutely wanted to make a good living, and I needed to support myself. How *would* I do that *now*?

Returning from Japan, I moved into my father's trailer in Taos, NM, to help him start a business at which he had been *massively* successful when he lived in Florida a few years back. He ran a newspaper for people who owned recreational vehicles (RVs). I had never stepped foot in an RV, never slept or driven in one, had no interest in them (I'm more of a tent camper myself), and never published a newspaper or sold ads before. None of that fazed me. My dad had owned an RV newspaper before, and now he wanted to come out of retirement. My mother had died, and I wanted to help my dad because I really loved him. So, off we went.

It was a disaster. I didn't know what I was doing, but I was fueled by the hunger to make the newspaper a success for myself, and especially for my father. His visionary side—once uncoupled from my mother's more pragmatic side—made him a walking bankruptcy about to ignite and burst into flames.

Here's what you would have seen if you could have peeped in…

First, my dad in a trailer, and me in his trailer with him. It was a lovely, double-wide place with lots of Taos mountain light and very comfortable. But it didn't seem right *at all*. My highly successful entrepreneurial father, in a lineage from *his* highly successful entrepreneurial father... this just didn't fit at all who I thought he was, or who I thought I was. I'm not a fancy person, and our life in Japan had been refreshingly simple and beautiful, but I admit this new life felt a bit weird to me. Yet, I felt impassioned about the business and helping him, and it relieved me because it gave me something to do for a living, something to at least try.

Once I arrived from Japan and moved in, I saw immediately that something was terribly, terribly wrong. Dad was spending money he didn't have, way before he was making it, and using the funds he raised from investors to support his business-related travel in a way that seemed very off and extravagant. Remember, I knew nothing at all about business, but we all have a sixth sense for when things are off, and this didn't take a psychic to suss out.

Let's fast forward a little. For many reasons, the business was *not* going well. I was the *only one successfully* selling ads, so I was the *only one* who was keeping us afloat, and we had staff, printing and shipping costs and much more. I was really worried. Dad concerned me the most. In fact, what I saw him doing, and *not* doing, absolutely terrified me.

Let's go back to what you would see on a usual day in his three-bedroom trailer, with the Taos light pouring in.

I got up and walked immediately to the narrow Parson's Bench, where there was a laptop on which I created the whole newspaper. All the ads, all the articles, all the photos–everything. I was still in my pajamas, and I hadn't brushed my teeth, showered, or eaten breakfast. I sat at that narrow table with my coffee, making calls and selling ads. I was listening to my father on the phone in the next room. I discovered that he worked and lived inside a massive ADHD confusion. He had not one ounce of ability to hold on to details he received, follow through, makes sales, and be able to put a roof over our heads. I made lists *for* him, but he couldn't even *remember* to actually *use* his lists! Yikes! How were we *ever* going to keep afloat – or have *any* income?

I was terrified. Every action I made, everything I did, was driven by sheer panic. Although four people were on the payroll, I was the only person producing at a level that could sustain us. I was creating from sheer desperation, *and I didn't even know that I was doing it.* I didn't feel like there was any other way. If you had told me at the time that there were other ways I could have done this, that I had other choices about what I was doing, or even how I was doing it, I wouldn't have believed you.

Sometime around 2 pm I would realize I was hungry, grab something to eat and *maybe* brush my teeth. Dressing and showering became optional. At least I would walk every day. Somehow that decades-old part of me, the Wendy who walked every day, never got lost. Thank goodness.

We also had Valdez, our beautiful gray striped cat, who would sit on our laps and purr, and keep my feet warm at night. Valdez was our one sane spot on the landscape.

I hired someone to 'guide' my dad, but even that wasn't enough. We were drowning. I'd hear him in the other room having warm conversations with prospective advertisers. Then at the end of the day, when I asked him how it went, he'd tell me what a lovely talk he'd had, and they were so nice on the phone. When I'd ask if he had *also* sold an ad, which is how we kept the paper alive and actually put food on the table, he would almost always say no.

In the meantime, crazy as it is, I was spending my own money— my savings—to keep the paper going. At least I was getting paid, right? Wrong. I didn't pay myself anything for most of the three years this madness went on. There wasn't enough money left over for me to be on the payroll. So, I was working myself crazy, acting like a mad woman, not paying myself, and spending my savings. By the way, I just looked up 'mad' as I wrote this, wanting to use another word. Here's what the Encarta online dictionary offered me in return: MAD: mutually assured destruction. Also: very unwise or rash. SO true. So true.

I continued for *three years,* running myself and my finances into the ground. I was panicked. I didn't see a way out. How *would* I make a living? I still refused to be a therapist. No matter what else was happening to me, no matter how scary it was, since all the therapies I knew didn't make the changes I wanted for myself or my clients, I still wasn't willing to reopen my practice.

With all that pressure and stress, almost zero self-care or perspective, no money coming in, and my savings gushing out, one day I found myself screaming at my dad. My parents hadn't really sworn when we were kids, or even after. The worst might have been "damn." They weren't overly proper; just a kind of civility that was more common back then. I only remember one time using a coarser word in front of my father. Swearing at him simply didn't feel right.

So, to hear myself *screaming* at him, in front of one of our staff members, made me cringe with embarrassment, shame, and despair. *I* had come to this. Even as I was screaming, I felt shame. I couldn't stop myself. I had become someone I never wanted to be. My center, who I am as a person, was unraveling. I knew it, and I couldn't stop.

As I slowly allowed myself to take in what my situation was, what *our* situation was, I realized I had to deal with letting go. Letting go of 'saving' my father, of 'saving' the paper, of 'saving' myself, and even of holding open a place in the business for my husband, so he could also return from Japan and have a way to make a living here. My shame and my fear took over for a time. I had to pry my fingers off what wasn't working. I had to massively open up to what I didn't want to see or feel.

I had lived for three years with the illusion and delusion that I was helping my father and that we *could* make this business work. The reality was darkly different. With great angst and terror, even while still thinking there *must* be a way…I let go. I insisted that we close the business. And I left.

I went to live on a 35' sloop sailboat in the Caribbean with my uncle and his wife for a few months to lick my wounds. This may seem like a strange solution for someone who gets seasick just leaving port, but that's another story of another shift that mattered.

I had let go of what I had thought would save me. I had let go of saving others. I had found a 'placeholder' way to make a living, but again, far from who I really am. I was desperate for input of a higher kind. I devoured the online world of transformation, spending tens of thousands of dollars on the next shiny object and the next shiny promise of instant wealth and making millions. I was besotted with the hype and fell for all of it.

I was still being crazy. MAD.

Yet, I *was* searching, earnestly, and I *did* have my sights firmly on a way to connect to a higher place, a higher guidance. I just had no idea how to get there.

Then one day, wanting to order a book from a publishing house, I mistakenly called the head of the Eidetics International Training Institute. Her number and the number of the publishing house were on the same card in my Rolodex (an ancient way of keeping people's information, pre-internet).

Eidetics is an ancient art and a 21st-century science. It works with the mind in a unique, out-of-the-box way. It's profoundly different from anything I have encountered in over forty years of working with and training in deep, inner transformational processes. I had heard about it *twenty years* before I made that 'mistaken' telephone call. But back then, I only trusted my conscious, overly rational mind. That meant that I was always in my head, and I couldn't drop into a deeper place in myself. I was using my rational, conscious mind to solve everything, including how to attain a more spiritual place inside myself, and it wasn't working. But I knew no other way.

The head of the Eidetics Training Institute invited me to attend an opening weekend workshop on Eidetics. It was an introduction for the three-year training in Connecticut, led by the father of Eidetics, Akhter Ahsen, Ph.D. Then, she offered the whipped cream on top. "Get yourself on a plane to New York City, take a cab to my house, and I will put you up, feed you, and drive you to Connecticut every day for the workshop."

How could I refuse?

This time, twenty years *after* I had first heard Dr. Ahsen speak, I was ready. His words entered my consciousness in a way that made my heart and mind race, but also breathe. As he worked with a small group of us, he took us through a process that seemed like the holy grail of transformational work. I was experiencing parts of myself—stuck and burdened parts—that I had never known were there, despite many years of inner 'work'.

I could feel the door open to the way out. I was delightedly hooked.

Although she was not a total stranger, it felt like a gift, like the kindness of strangers. I soaked it up. A larger consciousness had been speaking to me, but now I could hear more clearly. Thank you!

I jumped into the three-year training, flying several times a year from New Mexico to New York City for three-day trainings, opening my mind to another part of me. Opening up ways I had been 'insistently blind' to myself, and emerging as so much more of who I *really* am.

I began to hear and *feel* deep, consistent and beautiful guidance that came from way beyond my conscious, rational mind. By not seeing everything through the lens of my 'head', I was able to go deeper into myself, help my clients to be more of who *they* really are, and so much more.

I opened an international practice of Eidetics, working with my own personal Eidetic practitioner and high-level business coach. They led, and continue to lead me, decades later, through the traps of my mind and into a place where I *can and do* connect with myself, with something larger. It's a place in me that can thrive and grow, like a lotus emerging from the mud.

As the traps of the overly rational, overly cognitive parts of my mind opened, my husband returned home permanently from Japan. For years and years, early in our relationship, I was mentally divorcing him for hours every day. Now, I was determined to find a way to create a house of love. That house of love sits near national forest land on a 7,200' high mesa visited by bobcat, deer, dozens and dozens of swarming hummingbirds, and brilliantly feathered migrating warblers.

My schedule now supports *me*. Each morning I spend time with myself and nature before I turn on the computer to start work, breathing in the scrub oak and pinyon pine, and settling my mind before I begin my day. I have time and space to write, to create.

Inspirations and massive support are what I open myself too, and gratefully receive so often it makes my heart ache with awe.

My clients, my beautiful, open, so-very-willing private clients, value with their whole being who they get to be as they also let go of the traps of their overly rational minds. The effects of their changes ripple out into their work, the pace and breadth of their lives, their families, their children, and even their parents—both living and already gone. I get to make a difference, and I get to do it with the most beautiful transformational tool I have ever encountered, Eidetics.

I didn't stay with a successful private practice psychotherapy business because a part of me knew there was more. I didn't stay with trying to save my father, even though it took everything I had in me to leave when I still 'thought' it *might* work. I kept growing, even if slowly. When the student was ready, her teacher(s) appeared.

I was able to help my father live the rest of his days in comfort and safety without it costing me my life and my soul.

It took a journey from Houston to Japan to Thailand to Taos to Santa Fe and then Manhattan, but I couldn't have taken it if I hadn't ungripped my fingers from what wasn't working and trusted enough to let go.

Your shift matters: there really IS more to all of us than our overly rational minds want us to know. There really is more to *you* than what you currently 'think' is possible. If you are gripping, then this is especially true. Once you can at least *notice* the gripping, and what it is doing to you and your loved ones, you have a choice. You can choose the shift that matters. It may not feel possible; I know I didn't think I had a choice. But I did. And I hope you can see that you do, too. Because you *do* have that choice.

Conclusion

So, there you have it! Inspiring stories from amazing people who shifted from living a life of resistance to becoming truly resilient. I'm very proud of every author that contributed to this book. Their shifts have been nothing short of amazing!

They exposed their vulnerabilities so you can learn from their experiences. Some of these authors revealed parts of themselves they have never shown before. In part, it was because they knew that it would help them in their own healing process. However, mostly, they wanted to inspire you, the reader.

They wanted to show you that we all go through really tough, challenging times. It's not those times that matter, it's the lessons we learn along the way. Like the authors, you won't be given anything you can't handle.

It is my hope that you found a little bit of yourself in each of these stories and you realize that you, too, can enjoy life a heck of a lot more if you simply shift from living with resistance to becoming resilient. If you're suffering in some area of your life, there's nothing to be ashamed of, and there's nothing to fear. You can make that change. You've got this!

If you enjoyed this book, we'd all appreciate it if you'd hop on over to Amazon and write a review. This way the authors will know they did – indeed - have an impact! Thank you in advance for your support on this journey.

Remember, at the end of the day, in order to live your life all-in and full-out, *Your Shift Matters*.

To Your Shift,

Your *Shift* Matters

Shift ◆ Publish ◆ Profit

Are you an aspiring author? Perhaps you have a half-finished book stashed on your computer. Or maybe it's in a notebook that sits on your desk collecting dust. Worse yet, maybe you still haven't started your book despite all of the ideas that swim around in your head, and you think to yourself, *One day I'm going to write that book!*

You're not alone. Research shows that 80% of you reading this would like to be a published author one day. Unfortunately, a staggering 97% of you who start writing a book will never finish it!

Perhaps you:

- Want to write a book, but have no idea how to get started.

- Know there's a book inside of you, but the thought of writing overwhelms you.

- Have no idea how to publish a book.

- Don't know where to find editors, copy-writers, graphic designers, formatters, marketers, etc.

- Don't want to become an expert in publishing just to get your message to the masses.

I want YOU to be part of the 3% that finishes their book and gets published! Share your story, inspire people across the globe and leave a legacy for generations to come!

Visit <u>www.DanaZarcone.com</u> today!